The Newest Air Fryer

Recipes Cookbook UK

Yummy, Affordable & Super-Easy Air Fryer Recipes for Beginners and Advanced Users

Caitlin Naylor

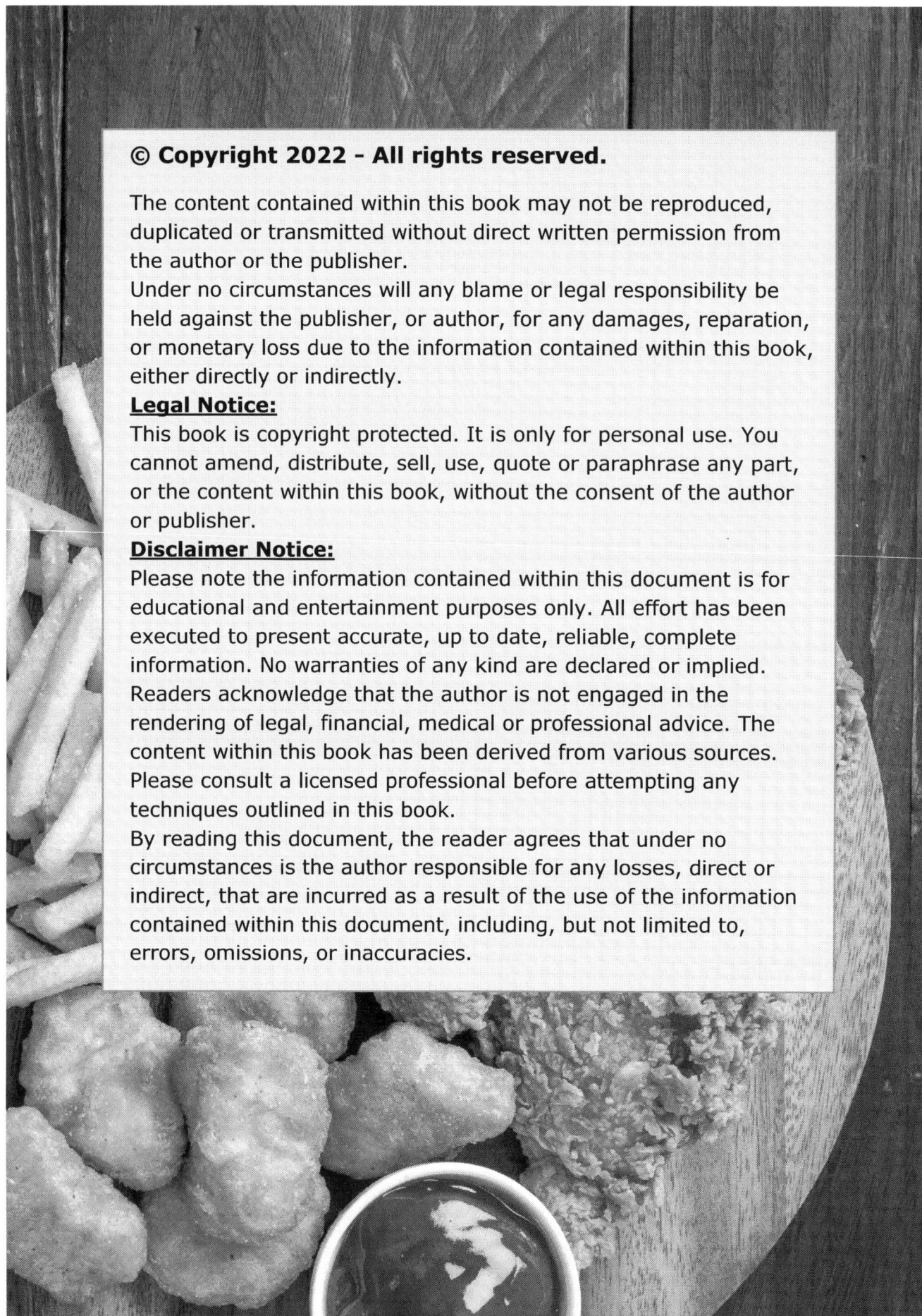

© Copyright 2022 - All rights reserved.

The content contained within this book may not be reproduced, duplicated or transmitted without direct written permission from the author or the publisher.

Under no circumstances will any blame or legal responsibility be held against the publisher, or author, for any damages, reparation, or monetary loss due to the information contained within this book, either directly or indirectly.

Legal Notice:

This book is copyright protected. It is only for personal use. You cannot amend, distribute, sell, use, quote or paraphrase any part, or the content within this book, without the consent of the author or publisher.

Disclaimer Notice:

Please note the information contained within this document is for educational and entertainment purposes only. All effort has been executed to present accurate, up to date, reliable, complete information. No warranties of any kind are declared or implied. Readers acknowledge that the author is not engaged in the rendering of legal, financial, medical or professional advice. The content within this book has been derived from various sources. Please consult a licensed professional before attempting any techniques outlined in this book.

By reading this document, the reader agrees that under no circumstances is the author responsible for any losses, direct or indirect, that are incurred as a result of the use of the information contained within this document, including, but not limited to, errors, omissions, or inaccuracies.

Table of Contents

Introduction 5
The Fundamentals of an Air Fryer 6
   What is an Air Fryer? 6
   Benefits of Using an Air Fryer 7
   A Step-by-Step Guide to Air Frying 8
   Cleaning and Caring for an Air Fryer 9
   Helpful Tips 9
   FAQs 9
4-Week Diet Plan 10
   Week 1 10
   Week 2 10
   Week 3 11
   Week 4 11
Breakfast Recipes 12
   Egg Bites 12
   Cheese Sausage Egg Bowl 12
   Sweet and Spicy Sausage 13
   Banana Muffins 13
   Simple Hash Browns 13
   Cheesy Baked Tater Tot 14
   Scramble Bacon Breakfast Casserole 14
   Sausage and Cheese Breakfast Biscuits .. 15
   Fried Chicken Wings and Waffles 15
   Air-Fried Potatoes 16
   Toast Sticks 16
   Tomato & Egg White Frittata 17
   Chocolate Scones 17
   Easy Blueberry Scones 18
   Banana Oatmeal 18
   Butter Blueberry Muffins 19
   Cream Cinnamon Rolls 19
   Oil-Free Fried Bacon 20
   Simple Cherry Tarts 20
   Grilled Ham and Cheese 21
   Tasty Hash Browns 21
   Cheese and Bacon Muffins 22
   Vanilla Strawberry Pastry 22
   Simple Bagels 23
   Golden Mini Potatoes 23
Vegetable and Side Recipes 24
   Potatoes Au Gratin 24
   Insalata Caprese 24
   Artichoke Hearts 25
   Lemon Broccoli 25
   Roasted Courgette and Red Peppers 25
   Parmesan Sweet Potatoes with Rosemary 26
   Citrusy Roasted Brussels Sprouts 26
   Crispy Crusted Artichoke Hearts 26
   Flavourful Green Tomatoes 27

   Parmesan Aubergine 27
   Four Cheese Macaroni 28
   Watermelon Salad 28
   Lemony Roasted Green Beans 29
   Honey Carrots and Walnuts 29
   Roasted Asparagus and Grape Tomatoes 29
   Greek Buffalo Cauliflower 30
   Spiced Kale Chips 30
   Brussels Sprouts with Honey-Sriracha
   Sauce 31
   Savory Sweet Potatoes 31
   Bacon and Cheese Rotini 32
   Lime Peppers 32
   Roasted Corn 33
   Glazed Carrots with Sweet Potatoes 33
Snack and Starter Recipes 34
   Cheeses Dip 34
   Cheddar Chicken Dip 34
   Cheese Pepperoni Rolls 34
   Tasty Courgette Fries 35
   Fried Ranch Pickle Spears 35
   Bacon Mozzarella Sticks 35
   Crispy Avocado Fries 36
   Hot Turkey Meatballs 36
   Salami Cheese Roll-Ups 36
   Garlic Crostini with Cheese 37
   Air-Fried Vegetable Spring Rolls 37
   Feta Courgette Roulades 38
   Roasted Herbed Tomatoes and Olives 38
   Simple Chips 39
   Cinnamon Apple Chips 39
   Cheese Cauliflower Buns 40
   Mini Spinach Meatballs 40
   Sweet Beef Jerky 41
   Mayonnaise Eggs 41
   Bacon-Wrapped Cabbage Bites with Sauce
   42
   Bacon Cauliflower Skewers 42
   Parmesan Chips 43
   Sausage-Stuffed Cremini Mushrooms 43
   Ranch Cauliflower Bites 44
   Ranch Chicken Bites 44
Fish and Seafood Recipes 45
   Fried Sardines with Dip 45
   Lemon Sea Bass 45
   Pesto Prawns with Pilaf 45
   Roasted Sea Bass with Vegetables 46
   Fish-Pork Sticks 46
   Homemade Ahi Tuna Steaks 46

Italian Marinara Cod Bake 47
Lemony Cod with Olives 47
Honey-Glazed Salmon Fillets 47
Simple and Quick Prawn 48
Chilli Garlic Prawn............................... 48
Crispy Coconut Prawn 48
Crab-Avocado Boats 49
Lemon-Butter Lobster Tails 49
Old Bay Tuna Cakes............................ 49
Baked Salmon Burgers with Broccoli Slaw 50
Baked Grouper with Tomatoes.............. 50
Steamed Cod with Swiss Chard 51
Fish Pitas with Yogurt......................... 51
Prawn Pasta with Mushrooms 52
Balsamic Prawn.................................. 52
Cajun Cod and Prawn Mango Salsa 53
Baked Salmon with Tomatoes 53
Pepper Trout with Lemon Wedges.......... 54
Prawn Pita... 54
Roasted Whole Red Snapper 55
Spiced Tuna Steaks 55
Crusted Cod 56
Tilapia Roulade 56

Poultry Recipes 57
Jerk Chicken Pepper Kebabs................. 57
Tangy Chicken Wings 57
Easy Chicken Breasts 57
Turmeric Chicken Thighs 58
Pecan-Crusted Chicken Breasts 58
Jumbo Chicken Meatballs..................... 58
Marinated Chicken Wings..................... 59
Gherkin Chicken Wings........................ 59
Ranch Chicken Meatballs 59
Chicken Thighs with Chunky Salsa 60
Onion Chicken Meatballs...................... 60
Strawberry–Glazed Chicken Tenders 60
Chicken Strawberries Salad.................. 61
Alfredo Chicken Breasts....................... 61
Spiced Chicken Legs 62
Buttermilk-Fried Marinated Chicken Thighs
.... 62
Thyme Chicken Tenders 63
Marinara Chicken Casserole 63
Spicy Chilli Chicken Drumsticks 64
Curry Chicken Legs............................. 64
Garlic Chicken Wings 65
Breaded Chicken Drumsticks................. 65
Chicken Wings in Fish Sauce 66
Yellow Mustard Wings 66

Cheese Chicken Patties 67
Chicken-Goat Cheese Balls 67
Chicken Bulgogi with Riced Cauliflower... 68

Beef, Pork, and Lamb Recipes 69
Flavourful Pork Ribs............................ 69
Tacos with Pineapple Salsa 69
Bacon and Cheese Ranch Pinwheels....... 70
Steak Quesadillas............................... 70
Chili Beef Bean Pie 71
Tacos with Pickled Radishes 71
Pork-Beef Meatballs............................ 72
Steak Salad....................................... 72
Worcestershire Pork Tenderloin 73
Citrusy Pork Ribs................................ 73
Tex-Mex Andouille Sausage 74
Pork Bratwurst and Sauerkraut 74
Miso-Glazed Pork Loin Roast 75
Cherry Pork Chops.............................. 75
Orange Pork over Rice 76
Roasted Dijon Pork Loin 76
Pork Bratwursts and Sauerkraut............ 77
Stuffed Pork Loins with Mushrooms........ 77
Delicious Cereal-Crusted Pork Chops 78
Vegetable-Stuffed Pork Loins 78
Fried Hangover Sandwiches 79
Pork Meatballs 79
Pork Cabbage Salad............................ 80
Chimichurri Flank Steak 81
Mustard Pork over Cauliflower Rice 82
Moo Shu Pork with Lettuce 83

Dessert Recipes................................ 84
Peanut Butter Cookies......................... 84
Orange Glazed Strawberry Cake............ 84
Blueberry Jars with Crumble Topping 85
Dark Chocolate Custard....................... 85
Lemony Kiwi Pavlova 86
Coco Rum Custard.............................. 86
Chocolate Cake 87
Cinnamon Chocolate Custard 87
Lime Almond Cake.............................. 88
Homemade Lemon Curd Palmiers 88
Chocolate Pavlova with Raspberries 89
Amaretto Cheesecake with Almonds....... 90
Strawberry Crumble Jars 91
Cheesecake with Blackberry Sauce 92
Lime Cheesecake 93

Conclusion 94
Appendix Air Fryer Cooking Chart........ 95

Introduction

Congratulations! You're the proud owner of an air fryer, a small countertop electrical appliance that cooks delicious and crispy food using little to no oil.
Now, your mind is probably full of questions. How does an air fryer work? Does it actually fry food? How do you clean and maintain an air fryer? How do you use it? You'll get all the vital information about these types of cookers here. We'll help you discover what food you can cook in an air fryer. Basically, you can prepare all types of food in one, but with less or no oil, and the texture will be the same as fried food.
Using an air fryer is an excellent way to prepare food in your kitchen without using too many utensils. You simply gather all your ingredients, perhaps do some peeling and chopping, and then throw them into the air fryer. Adjust the cooking time and temperature according to the recipe instructions. The result? You'll have delicious and satisfying food with little to no effort.
From breakfasts to side dishes, mains, and desserts, you can cook all types of meals using an air fryer. It's pretty simple to use, and all buttons are user-friendly. The cleaning method is also incredibly easy. Just make sure you don't put the whole appliance into the dishwasher.
You'll get to spend more time with your family than in the kitchen,   plus you'll feed them delicious, nutritious food. An air fryer is a perfect companion for busy people everywhere. Let's jump into everything you need to know about your new air fryer.

The Fundamentals of an Air Fryer

The air fryer cooks food by circulating hot air around it. One of its main benefits is its numerous cooking functions. It doesn't just fry food; it can bake and roast it. This handy appliance not only bakes cookies, cakes, and brownies but will create a scrumptious roast dinner, too. The best part? The air fryer cooks food with little to no oil. Plus, you don't need to spend ages washing up numerous pots, pans, baking trays, or bowls. Simply gather all your ingredients and prepare them. Throw them into the air fryer. Adjust the cooking time and temperature according to your recipe. Wait until the appliance beeps and your meal is ready to be served. The air fryer comes with all the essential accessories you'll need. You don't need to purchase a basket, baking tray, or other items. Simply put, an air fryer is simple to use and simple to clean!

What is an Air Fryer?

An air fryer is a user-friendly cooking appliance, easily used by anyone. It usually has seven cooking functions: crisp, fry, roast, grill, reheat, bake and dehydrate. It has simple-to-use operating buttons to control temperature, cooking time, start/stop, and power. The air fryer comes with useful accessories such as a reversible rack, air fryer basket, dehydrating rack, etc. By using its various programs, you can cook your favourite foods like French fries, pizza, casseroles, tacos, cakes, cookies, brownies, etc.
The air fryer has become a global phenomenon. In this cookbook, I've added air fryer recipes for the UK. All the ingredients are readily available in supermarkets and are written in UK measurements. The air fryer is the top trending appliance because of its health benefits and remarkable features. Now, let's look in more detail at its benefits!

Benefits of Using an Air Fryer

There are lots of benefits to using air fryer cooking appliances. These benefits include:

Food is cooked in very little to no oil:
The main advantage of this appliance is that it cooks food with little to no oil, leading to numerous health benefits. It's also an excellent choice for people looking to lose weight or reduce their fat intake.

Pretty simple cleaning process:
The air fryer comes with removable cooking parts. Before cleaning, you can remove them all and put them into the dishwasher. But remember: don't put the main unit in the dishwasher or submerge it in water. Doing so will damage your appliance. You can wipe the main unit with a damp cloth. When all the parts are dry, reassemble the unit.

Fast and safe:
The air fryer is an advanced cooking gadget. It cooks faster than other appliances and even the hob or oven. It's safe to use, doesn't produce too much steam or heat, and doesn't risk splashing oil like deep-fat fryers. You can adjust the cooking time and temperature according to the recipe instructions. The air fryer has a control panel with pre-set and user-friendly buttons, and you can adjust the time and temperature there.

No stove or oven needed:
An air fryer offers all types of cooking functions. You no longer need a stove or oven to bake or roast food; this handy appliance can even grill, fry, and dehydrate food.

Minimal mess:
When you use an air fryer, you'll discover that our kitchen will be easier to clean – no splattering oil or multiple dirty pans or trays to wash. And the air fryer basket is simple to clean as it's virtually non-stick and dishwasher-safe.

The perfect companion for busy people:
The air fryer is a perfect addition to your kitchen and offers simple cooking with minimal effort. Prepare the ingredients and add them to the air fryer basket. Adjust the cooking time, temperature, and desired functions and start cooking.

Large capacity:
The air fryer has a large capacity, meaning you can cook meals for the whole family. You can even roast an entire turkey for Christmas Day!

Time and money-saving:
An air fryer is ideal for cooking food in less time. It also saves you money; with an air fryer, you can make your favourite restaurant dishes or takeaway meals without the cost. Plus, you'll make these meals healthier by using less oil and ensuring your ingredients are freshly prepared.

A Step-by-Step Guide to Air Frying

First, clean it:
If you're using your air fryer for the first time, you'll need to ensure you clean it thoroughly. First, remove all packaging and labels from the appliance. Also, remove any accessories. Wash the air fryer basket and cooking tray in the dishwasher or hand wash them with warm soapy water. Clean the main unit inside and out with a soft cloth. When everything is dry, reassemble the appliance.

Choose a recipe from this cookbook:
Choose a recipe that catches your eye from this cookbook. I've included all types of recipes: Breakfast, Lunch, Dinner, Dessert, Snacks, etc. Have a good read through the book before picking a recipe you'd like to start with.

Buy fresh ingredients only:
It's a good idea to buy fresh ingredients, spices, veggies, fruits, and meat to get the best results. And buying fresh is better for your health too. Ensure you rinse all fruit and veg before cooking them.

Prepare the ingredients:
Before cooking, gather all your ingredients and measure them according to the recipe instructions. Try to cut veggies to the same size to ensure they cook evenly. If you want to marinate meat, do so in advance. If you're using frozen food, allow it to thaw if needed.

Preheat the unit if needed:
Some air fryer models need preheating, usually for the baking, roasting, and air frying functions. Please read the instructions carefully for your appliance and preheat it accordingly.

Spray the food with non-stick cooking spray:
Use high-quality cooking spray to spray your food before seasoning it. This will allow the seasoning to stick to the food and ensure that no smoke will be emitted from the appliance.

Select the cooking time, temperature, and desired cooking functions:
Select your desired function (such as Air Fry). Select the temperature and cooking time according to the recipe instructions. Place the food into the air fryer basket, baking dish, or cooking tray and close the lid/door of the main unit.

Flip the food if needed:
Some recipes will require food to be flipped over during cooking time. Some air fryer models will notify you when you need to turn your food. If not, you'll need to remember to do so yourself. Open the main unit's lid, shake the basket (or stir the food on the baking dish/tray), and close the lid. The cooking time will pause when you open the lid, and it will resume after closing it.

Remove the food when cooking time is complete:
Most air fryers' displays will let you know when the cooking time is complete. Remove the basket or tray from the appliance, then remove the food and transfer it to serving plates. Remember, the food will be piping hot!

Clean the air fryer after every use:
The air fryer basket is made with a non-stick coating and is dishwasher-safe. Rinse it under warm and soapy water first to remove any residue. Allow the appliance to cool before removing all accessories for cleaning.

Cleaning and Caring for an Air Fryer

Cleaning an air fryer is pretty simple. There are some instructions you should follow to maintain the appliance:

• Utensils such as steel wire brushes, metal utensils, and abrasive sponges can damage the surface of the main unit. Don't use them to remove leftover food from the air fryer basket, as it can damage the surface.
• Don't put the main unit into the dishwasher, as it will damage it beyond repair.
• Before cleaning, unplug the main unit from the socket. Don't immerse the unit in water.
• Clean the air fryer after every use. All parts of the air fryer are removable. Before cleaning, allow the main unit to cool, then remove the accessories using oven gloves or tongs.
• Use a damp cloth or non-abrasive sponge to clean the main unit's interior and exterior.
• To remove the grease from the air fryer basket, soak it overnight in warm soapy water.
• Use a soft scrub brush, washing-up liquid, baking soda, and a clean cloth for deep cleaning.

To deep clean:
• Unplug the appliance and allow it to cool for 30 minutes. Remove the pan and basket from the air fryer and wash them with hot water and soap. If you see grease on these parts, soak them in hot water for 10 minutes. Then, scrub with a non-abrasive sponge.
• Clean the basket's interior with washing-up liquid and wipe it with a damp cloth.
• Wipe the appliance with a moist or damp cloth carefully.
• If you see stubborn residue on the basket, mix baking soda and water and scrub the mixture into the grime with a soft brush.
• When all parts are dry, return them to the main unit.
• Reassemble the air fryer before the next use.

Helpful Tips

• Preheat the appliance according to the manufacturer's instructions. Add the food to the basket in one layer to produce tender and evenly-cooked food.
• For best results, remove food from the air fryer immediately after cooking to avoid burning and overcooking.
• Don't touch the surface of the main unit while cooking food. Use oven mitts or tongs. Remove the air fryer basket with oven mitts.
• Adjust the desired temperature and cooking time on the display screen. Press the start/stop button to start or stop cooking.
• When you open the lid during cooking, the cooking time will pause. When you close the top, the cooking time will resume.
• Use 1 tablespoon of oil for cooking vegetables.
• Flip the food if required by the recipe.
• Don't overfill the basket.
• Remove excess water from your ingredients, or the appliance will produce smoke.

FAQs

Why isn't the air fryer turning on?
Answer: Plug the appliance into another socket. Ensure that it's plugged in well.
Why does my air fryer shut off?
Answer: If you don't choose a cooking function within 10 minutes, the unit will turn off automatically.

4-Week Diet Plan

Week 1

Day 1:
Breakfast: Egg Bites
Lunch: Parmesan Aubergine
Snack: Ranch Cauliflower Bites
Dinner: Pesto Prawns with Pilaf
Dessert: Peanut Butter Cookies

Day 2:
Breakfast: Tomato & Egg White Frittata
Lunch: Glazed Carrots with Sweet Potatoes
Snack: Fried Ranch Pickle Spears
Dinner: Chili Beef Bean Pie
Dessert: Orange Glazed Strawberry Cake

Day 3:
Breakfast: Easy Blueberry Scones
Lunch: Savory Sweet Potatoes
Snack: Salami Cheese Roll-Ups
Dinner: Easy Chicken Breasts
Dessert: Lime Almond Cake

Day 4:
Breakfast: Butter Blueberry Muffins
Lunch: Spiced Kale Chips
Snack: Crispy Avocado Fries
Dinner: Chilli Garlic Prawn
Dessert: Chocolate Cake

Day 5:
Breakfast: Air-Fried Potatoes
Lunch: Roasted Asparagus and Grape Tomatoes
Snack: Parmesan Chips
Dinner: Cherry Pork Chops
Dessert: Blueberry Jars with Crumble Topping

Day 6:
Breakfast: Sausage and Cheese Breakfast Biscuits
Lunch: Lemony Roasted Green Beans
Snack: Simple Chips
Dinner: Curry Chicken Legs
Dessert: Cinnamon Chocolate Custard

Day 7:
Breakfast: Cheesy Baked Tater Tot
Lunch: Citrusy Roasted Brussels Sprouts
Snack: Garlic Crostini with Cheese
Dinner: Worcestershire Pork Tenderloin
Dessert: Lemony Kiwi Pavlova

Week 2

Day 1:
Breakfast: Grilled Ham and Cheese
Lunch: Roasted Courgette and Red Peppers
Snack: Feta Courgette Roulades
Dinner: Prawn Pita
Dessert: Chocolate Pavlova with Raspberries

Day 2:
Breakfast: Cheese and Bacon Muffins
Lunch: Artichoke Hearts
Snack: Bacon-Wrapped Cabbage Bites with Sauce
Dinner: Pork Bratwursts and Sauerkraut
Dessert: Amaretto Cheesecake with Almonds

Day 3:
Breakfast: Simple Bagels
Lunch: Bacon and Cheese Rotini
Snack: Sweet Beef Jerky
Dinner: Tangy Chicken Wings
Dessert: Strawberry Crumble Jars

Day 4:
Breakfast: Golden Mini Potatoes
Lunch: Four Cheese Macaroni
Snack: Cheese Cauliflower Buns
Dinner: Italian Marinara Cod Bake
Dessert: Lime Cheesecake

Day 5:
Breakfast: Toast Sticks
Lunch: Potatoes Au Gratin
Snack: Cheddar Chicken Dip
Dinner: Tex-Mex Andouille Sausage
Dessert: Cheesecake with Blackberry Sauce

Day 6:
Breakfast: Simple Hash Browns
Lunch: Flavourful Green Tomatoes
Snack: Cheeses Dip
Dinner: Garlic Chicken Wings
Dessert: Dark Chocolate Custard

Day 7:
Breakfast: Cheese Sausage Egg Bowl
Lunch: Roasted Corn
Snack: Cheese Pepperoni Rolls
Dinner: Crab-Avocado Boats
Dessert: Coco Rum Custard

Week 3

Day 1:
Breakfast: Chocolate Scones
Lunch: Brussels Sprouts with Honey-Sriracha Sauce
Snack: Mini Spinach Meatballs
Dinner: Pork-Beef Meatballs
Dessert: Homemade Lemon Curd Palmiers

Day 2:
Breakfast: Banana Oatmeal
Lunch: Greek Buffalo Cauliflower
Snack: Mayonnaise Eggs
Dinner: Cheese Chicken Patties
Dessert: Peanut Butter Cookies

Day 3:
Breakfast: Cream Cinnamon Rolls
Lunch: Honey Carrots and Walnuts
Snack: Bacon Cauliflower Skewers
Dinner: Fried Sardines with Dip
Dessert: Orange Glazed Strawberry Cake

Day 4:
Breakfast: Simple Cherry Tarts
Lunch: Crispy Crusted Artichoke Hearts
Snack: Roasted Herbed Tomatoes and Olives
Dinner: Steak Quesadillas
Dessert: Lime Almond Cake

Day 5:
Breakfast: Fried Chicken Wings and Waffles
Lunch: Parmesan Sweet Potatoes with Rosemary
Snack: Air-Fried Vegetable Spring Rolls
Dinner: Pork Cabbage Salad
Dessert: Chocolate Cake

Day 6:
Breakfast: Scramble Bacon Breakfast Casserole
Lunch: Lemon Broccoli
Snack: Cinnamon Apple Chips
Dinner: Fish-Pork Sticks
Dessert: Blueberry Jars with Crumble Topping

Day 7:
Breakfast: Tasty Hash Browns
Lunch: Lime Peppers
Snack: Sausage-Stuffed Cremini Mushrooms
Dinner: Chicken Strawberries Salad
Dessert: Cinnamon Chocolate Custard

Week 4

Day 1:
Breakfast: Vanilla Strawberry Pastry
Lunch: Watermelon Salad
Snack: Hot Turkey Meatballs
Dinner: Vegetable-Stuffed Pork Loins
Dessert: Lemony Kiwi Pavlova

Day 2:
Breakfast: Oil-Free Fried Bacon
Lunch: Insalata Caprese
Snack: Tasty Courgette Fries
Dinner: Baked Salmon with Tomatoes
Dessert: Chocolate Pavlova with Raspberries

Day 3:
Breakfast: Sweet and Spicy Sausage
Lunch: Potatoes Au Gratin
Snack: Bacon Mozzarella Sticks
Dinner: Pecan-Crusted Chicken Breasts
Dessert: Amaretto Cheesecake with Almonds

Day 4:
Breakfast: Banana Muffins
Lunch: Four Cheese Macaroni
Snack: Ranch Chicken Bites
Dinner: Roasted Dijon Pork Loin
Dessert: Strawberry Crumble Jars

Day 5:
Breakfast: Egg Bites
Lunch: Bacon and Cheese Rotini
Snack: Cheese Pepperoni Rolls
Dinner: Fish Pitas with Yogurt
Dessert: Lime Cheesecake

Day 6:
Breakfast: Tomato & Egg White Frittata
Lunch: Artichoke Hearts
Snack: Bacon-Wrapped Cabbage Bites with Sauce
Dinner: Alfredo Chicken Breasts
Dessert: Cheesecake with Blackberry Sauce

Day 7:
Breakfast: Butter Blueberry Muffins
Lunch: Roasted Courgette and Red Peppers
Snack: Feta Courgette Roulades
Dinner: Bacon and Cheese Ranch Pinwheels
Dessert: Dark Chocolate Custard

Breakfast Recipes

Egg Bites

Prep Time: 5 minutes | **Cook Time:** 9 minutes | **Serves:** 2

2 large eggs
50g full-fat cottage cheese
25g shredded sharp Cheddar cheese
¼ teaspoon salt
⅛ teaspoon ground black pepper
6 tablespoons diced cooked ham

1. Preheat the air fryer to 150°C. Spray six silicone muffin cups with cooking spray. 2. Add the eggs, cottage cheese, Cheddar, salt, and pepper to the blender, and pulse them five times until smooth and frothy. 3. Place 1 tablespoon ham in the bottom of each prepared baking cup, then divide the egg mixture among cups. 4. Place the muffin cups in the air fryer basket and cook for 9 minutes until egg bites are firm in the centre. 5. Carefully remove cups from air fryer basket and cool them for 3 minutes before serving. Serve warm.
Per Serving: Calories 260; Fat 18.37g; Sodium 822mg; Carbs 5.08g; Fibre 1.1g; Sugar 1.17g; Protein 18.55g

Cheese Sausage Egg Bowl

Prep Time: 5 minutes | **Cook Time:** 15 minutes | **Serves:** 4

6 large eggs
2 tablespoons heavy cream
½ teaspoon salt
¼ teaspoon ground black pepper
60g crumbled pork sausage, cooked and drained
50g shredded Cheddar cheese

1. Preheat the air fryer to 160°C. Spray a 15 cm round cake pan with cooking spray. 2. Whisk eggs, cream, salt, and pepper in a bowl until fully combined. 3. Arrange the cooked sausage, egg mixture and cheese on the cake pan in order, then cook them in the air fryer for 15 minutes until the top begins to brown and the centre is set. 4. Let the food cool for 5 minutes. Serve warm.
Per Serving: Calories 373; Fat 29.23g; Sodium 1292mg; Carbs 1.63g; Fibre 0g; Sugar 0.68g; Protein 24.43g

Sweet and Spicy Sausage

Prep Time: 5 minutes | **Cook Time:** 10 minutes | **Serves:** 6

455g lean pork mince
2 tablespoons brown sugar
1 teaspoon salt
½ teaspoon ground black pepper
½ teaspoon garlic powder
½ teaspoon dried fennel
½ teaspoon crushed red pepper flakes

1. Preheat the air fryer to 200°C. 2. Mix all ingredients in a large bowl. Divide mixture into eight portions and form into patties. 3. Spritz patties with cooking spray and place in the air fryer basket. Cook them for 10 minutes until patties are brown and internal temperature reaches at least 60°C. 4. Serve warm.
Per Serving: Calories 106; Fat 3.07g; Sodium 439mg; Carbs 3.81g; Fibre 0.2g; Sugar 3g; Protein 16.17g

Banana Muffins

Prep Time: 5 minutes | **Cook Time:** 15 minutes | **Serves:** 12

190g plain flour
95g granulated sugar
1 teaspoon baking powder
115g salted butter, melted
1 large egg
2 medium bananas, peeled and mashed
60g chopped pecans

1. Preheat the air fryer to 150°C. 2. In a large bowl, whisk the flour, sugar, and baking powder. 3. Add butter, egg, and bananas, and stir until well combined and thick. 4. Gently fold in pecans. Divide batter evenly among twelve silicone or aluminum muffin cups, filling cups about halfway full. 5. Place cups in the air fryer basket, working in batches as necessary. Cook them for 15 minutes until muffin edges are brown and a toothpick inserted into the centre comes out clean. 6. Let cool 5 minutes before serving.
Per Serving: Calories 169; Fat 8.67g; Sodium 43mg; Carbs 21.39g; Fibre 1.3g; Sugar 6.7g; Protein 2.49g

Simple Hash Browns

Prep Time: 5 minutes | **Cook Time:** 30 minutes | **Serves:** 2

2 large russet potatoes, peeled
480ml cold water
1 tablespoon olive oil
½ teaspoon salt

1. Grate potatoes into a bowl filled with cold water, and soak them for 10 minutes. 2. Drain them into a colander, then press into paper towels to remove excess moisture. 3. Dry the bowl and return potatoes to it. Toss with oil and salt. 4. Preheat the air fryer to 190°C. Spray a suitable cake pan with cooking spray. 5. Place potatoes in the prepared pan, pressing them down. 6. Cook the potatoes for 20 minutes until brown and crispy. 7. Serve warm.
Per Serving: Calories 228; Fat 6.92g; Sodium 597mg; Carbs 38.49g; Fibre 2.8g; Sugar 1.32g; Protein 4.56g

Cheesy Baked Tater Tot

Prep time: 5 minutes| **Cook time:** 20 minutes| **Serves:** 4

4 eggs
240ml milk
1 teaspoon onion powder
Salt
Pepper
Cooking oil
340g ground chicken sausage
450g frozen tater tots
85g shredded Cheddar cheese

1. In a medium bowl, whisk the eggs. Add the milk, onion powder, salt, and pepper to taste. Stir to combine. 2. Spray a skillet with cooking oil and set over medium-high heat. Add the ground sausage. Using a spatula or spoon, break the sausage into smaller pieces. Cook for 3 to 4 minutes until the sausage is brown. Remove from heat and set aside. 3. Spray a barrel pan with cooking oil. Make sure to cover the bottom and sides of the pan. 4. Place the tater tots in the barrel pan. Cook for 6 minutes. 5. Open the air fryer and shake the pan, then add the egg mixture and cooked sausage. Cook at 400°F/ 200°C for an additional 6 minutes. 6. Open the air fryer and sprinkle the cheese over the tater tot bake. Cook for an additional 2 to 3 minutes. Cool before serving.
Per Serving: Calories 525; Fat 29.8g; Sodium 389mg; Carbs 30.3g; Fibre 0.3g; Sugar 27g; Protein 34.5g

Scramble Bacon Breakfast Casserole

Prep time: 20 minutes| **Cook time:** 10 minutes| **Serves:** 4

6 slices bacon
6 eggs
Salt
Pepper
Cooking oil
35g chopped red pepper
35g chopped green pepper
60g chopped onion
85g cup shredded Cheddar cheese

1. Set a skillet over medium-high heat, and then cook the bacon for 5 to 7 minutes, flipping to ensure even crispiness. Drain on paper towels, crumble, and set aside. 2. In a medium bowl, whisk the eggs. Add salt and pepper to taste. 3. Spray a barrel pan with cooking oil. Make sure to cover the bottom and sides of the pan. 4. Add the beaten eggs, crumbled bacon, red pepper, green pepper, and onion to the pan. Place the pan in the air fryer. Cook the mixture at 400°F/ 200°C for 6 minutes. 5. Open the air fryer and sprinkle the cheese over the casserole. Cook for an additional 2 minutes. Cool before serving.
Per Serving: Calories 370; Fat 30g; Sodium 707mg; Carbs 5.8g; Fibre 0.8g; Sugar 3g; Protein 19g

Sausage and Cheese Breakfast Biscuits

Prep time: 5 minutes| **Cook time:** 15 minutes| **Serves:** 5

340g chicken breakfast sausage
1 (170g) can biscuits
30g cream cheese

1. Form the sausage into 5 small patties. 2. Place the sausage patties in the air fryer. Cook at 370°F/ 185°C for 5 minutes. 3. Open the air fryer. Flip the patties. Cook for an additional 5 minutes. Remove the cooked sausages from the air fryer. 4. Separate the biscuit dough into 5 biscuits. Place the biscuits in the air fryer. Cook at 370°F/ 185°C for 3 minutes. 5. Open the air fryer. Flip the biscuits. Cook for an additional 2 minutes. 6. Remove the cooked biscuits from the air fryer. 7. Split each biscuit in half. Spread 1 teaspoon of cream cheese onto the bottom of each biscuit. Top with a sausage patty and the other half of the biscuit, and serve.
Per Serving: Calories 116; Fat 7.3g; Sodium 68mg; Carbs 0.25g; Fibre 0g; Sugar 0.2g; Protein 12.3g

Fried Chicken Wings and Waffles

Prep time: 10 minutes| **Cook time:** 30 minutes| **Serves:** 4

8 whole chicken wings
1 teaspoon garlic powder
Chicken seasoning or rub
Pepper
60g all-purpose flour
Cooking oil
8 frozen waffles
Maple syrup (optional)

1. In a medium bowl, season the chicken with the garlic powder and chicken seasoning and pepper to taste. 2. Transfer the chicken wings to a sealable plastic bag and add the flour. Shake to thoroughly coat the chicken. 3. Spray the air fryer basket with cooking oil. 4. Using tongs, transfer the chicken wings from the bag to the air fryer. It is okay to stack the chicken wings on top of each other. Spray them with cooking oil. Cook at 400°F/ 200°C for 5 minutes. 5. Open the air fryer and shake the basket. Continue to cook the chicken. Repeat shaking every 5 minutes until 20 minutes has passed and the chicken is fully cooked. 6. Remove the cooked chicken from the air fryer and set it aside. 7. Rinse the basket and base out with warm water. Return them to the air fryer. Reduce the temperature of the air fryer to 370°F/ 185°C. 8. Place the frozen waffles in the air fryer. Do not stack. Depending on the size of your air fryer, you may need to cook the waffles in batches. Spray the waffles with cooking oil. Cook at 370°F/ 185°C for 6 minutes. If necessary, remove the cooked waffles from the air fryer, then repeat the cooking steps for the remaining waffles. 9. Serve the waffles with the chicken and a touch of maple syrup if desired.
Per Serving: Calories 338; Fat 9g; Sodium 505mg; Carbs 43.7g; Fibre 2.2g; Sugar 4g; Protein 19.4g

Air-Fried Potatoes

Prep time: 35 minutes| **Cook time:** 25 minutes| **Serves:** 4

3 large russet potatoes
1 tablespoon canola oil
1 tablespoon extra-virgin olive oil
1 teaspoon paprika
Salt
Pepper
120g chopped onion
75g chopped red pepper
75g chopped green pepper

1. Cut the potatoes into ½-inch cubes. Soak the potatoes in a large bowl of cold water for at least 30 minutes, preferably an hour. 2. Then drain the bowl and dry the potatoes thoroughly with paper towels. Return them to the empty bowl. 3. Add the canola oil and olive oil, paprika, and salt and pepper to taste. Toss to fully coat the potatoes. 4. Place the potatoes in the air fryer and cook at 370°F/ 185°C for 20 minutes, shaking the air fryer basket every 5 minutes (a total of 4 times). 5. Place the onion and bell peppers in the air fryer basket. Cook for an additional 3 to 4 minutes or until the potatoes are cooked through, and the peppers are soft. Cool before serving.
Per Serving: Calories 309; Fat 7.3g; Sodium 18mg; Carbs 56.5g; Fibre 5g; Sugar 5g; Protein 7g

Toast Sticks

Prep Time: 5 minutes | **Cook Time:** 8 minutes | **Serves:** 4

4 slices thick-sliced bread
2 large eggs
60g heavy cream
4 tablespoons salted butter, melted
95g granulated sugar
1½ tablespoons ground cinnamon

1. Preheat the air fryer to 175°C. Cut parchment paper to fit the air fryer basket. 2. Slice each piece of bread into four even sticks. 3. Beat the eggs with cream in a medium bowl. 4. Dip each bread stick into mixture, and place them in the air fryer basket. 5. Cook them for 5 minutes, then carefully turn over and cook an additional 3 minutes until golden brown on both sides. 6. Drizzle sticks with butter and toss to ensure they're covered on all sides. 7. Mix sugar and cinnamon in another bowl. Dip both sides of each stick into the mixture and shake off excess. 8. Serve warm.
Per Serving: Calories 238; Fat 13.48g; Sodium 199mg; Carbs 25.11g; Fibre 2.1g; Sugar 13.73g; Protein 5.26g

Tomato & Egg White Frittata

Prep Time: 5 minutes | **Cook Time:** 8 minutes | **Serves:** 2

485g liquid egg whites
15g chopped fresh spinach
45g chopped tomato
½ teaspoon salt
20g chopped white onion

1. Preheat the air fryer to 160°C. Spray a 15 cm round baking dish with cooking spray. 2. Whisk egg whites in a large bowl until frothy, and then mix with the spinach, tomato, salt, and onion. 3. Pour egg mixture into prepared dish, and cook 8 minutes until the centre is set. 4. Serve warm.
Per Serving: Calories 158; Fat 1.53g; Sodium 1036mg; Carbs 6.83g; Fibre 0.8g; Sugar 2.55g; Protein 27.23g

Chocolate Scones

Prep Time: 15 minutes | **Cook Time:** 15 minutes | **Serves:** 8

115g cold salted butter, divided
250g plain flour
110g brown sugar
½ teaspoon baking powder
1 large egg
85g semisweet chocolate chips

1. Preheat the air fryer to 160°C. Cut parchment paper to fit the air fryer basket. 2. Chill 6 tablespoons butter in the freezer for 10 minutes. 3. Add the remaining butter to a small microwave-safe bowl, and microwave for 30 seconds until melted, and then set aside. 4. Mix the flour, brown sugar, and baking powder in a large bowl. 5. Remove butter from freezer and grate into bowl. Use a wooden spoon to evenly distribute; add egg and buttermilk, and stir gently until a sticky dough forms. Gently fold in chocolate chips. 6. Turn dough out onto a lightly floured surface. Fold a couple of times and gently form into a 15 cm round. Cut into eight triangles. 7. Place scones on parchment in the air fryer basket, leaving at least 5 cm space between each (you can cook in batches). 8. Brush each scone with melted butter, then cook them for 15 minutes until scones are dark golden brown and crispy on the edges, and a toothpick inserted into the centre comes out clean. 9. Serve warm.
Per Serving: Calories 304; Fat 12g; Sodium 121mg; Carbs 45.54g; Fibre 1.5g; Sugar 20.45g; Protein 5.32g

Easy Blueberry Scones

Prep Time: 15 minutes | **Cook Time:** 15 minutes | **Serves:** 8

115g cold salted butter, divided
250g plain flour
95g granulated sugar
1 teaspoon baking powder
1 large egg
120ml whole milk
75g fresh blueberries

1. Chill 6 tablespoons of butter in the freezer 10 minutes. Add the remaining butter to a small microwave-safe bowl, and microwave for 30 seconds until melted. 2. Preheat the air fryer to 160°C. Cut parchment paper to fit the air fryer basket. 3. In a large bowl, mix flour, sugar, and baking powder. 4. Add egg and milk and stir until a sticky dough forms. 5. Remove butter from freezer and grate into bowl. Fold grated butter into dough until just combined; fold in blueberries. 6. Lightly flour the work surface, place the dough on it, sprinkle dough with flour and fold a couple of times, then gently form the dough into a 15 cm round. Cut into eight triangles. 7. Place scones on parchment in the air fryer basket, leaving at least 5 cm of space between each, working in batches as necessary. 8. Brush each scone with melted butter, and cook them for 15 minutes until scones are dark golden brown and crispy on the edges, and a toothpick inserted into the centre comes out clean. 9. Serve warm.
Per Serving: Calories 241; Fat 9.05g; Sodium 72mg; Carbs 35.96g; Fibre 1.1g; Sugar 11.45g; Protein 4.2g

Banana Oatmeal

Prep Time: 5 minutes | **Cook Time:** 10 minutes | **Serves:** 2

80g quick-cooking oats
240ml whole milk
2 tablespoons unsalted butter, melted
1 medium banana, peeled and mashed
2 tablespoons brown sugar
½ teaspoon vanilla extract
½ teaspoon salt

1. Preheat the air fryer to 180°C. 2. Add the oats, milk and butter to a suitable pan. 3. Mix banana, brown sugar, vanilla, and salt in a bowl until combined, then add them to pan and mix until well combined. 4. Cook them in the preheated air fryer 10 minutes until the top is brown and oats feel firm to the touch. 5. Serve warm.
Per Serving: Calories 310; Fat 12.6g; Sodium 642mg; Carbs 49.87g; Fibre 4.4g; Sugar 31.11g; Protein 8.25g

Butter Blueberry Muffins

Prep Time: 5 minutes | **Cook Time:** 15 minutes | **Serves:** 12

125g plain flour
95g granulated sugar
1 teaspoon baking powder
60g salted butter, melted
1 large egg
120ml whole milk
150g fresh blueberries

1. Preheat the air fryer to 150°C. 2. In a large bowl, Whisk the flour, sugar, and baking powder in a large bowl, then stir in the butter, egg, and milk until combined; gently fold in blueberries. 3. Divide batter evenly among twelve silicone or aluminum muffin cups, filling cups about halfway full. 4. Cook the muffins in the air fryer for 15 minutes until muffins are brown at the edges and a toothpick inserted in the centre comes out clean (you can cook them in batches). 5. Serve warm.
Per Serving: Calories 111; Fat 3.44g; Sodium 32mg; Carbs 18.35g; Fibre 0.6g; Sugar 9.79g; Protein 2.07g

Cream Cinnamon Rolls

Prep Time: 10 minutes | **Cook Time:** 12 minutes | **Serves:** 8

1 sheet frozen puff pastry, thawed
6 tablespoons unsalted butter, melted
170g granulated sugar
2 tablespoons ground cinnamon
60g icing sugar
2 tablespoons heavy cream

1. Preheat the air fryer to 160°C. Cut parchment paper to fit the air fryer basket. 2. Unroll puff pastry into a large rectangle, and brush with butter, then evenly coat the dough with sugar and cinnamon. 3. Starting at one of the long sides, roll dough into a log, then use a little water on your fingers to seal the edge. 4. Cut the dough into eight rounds, and then transfer them to the air fryer basket. 5. Cook them for 12 minutes until golden brown and flaky. 6. Let them cool 5 minutes after cooking. 7. Whisk icing sugar and cream in a small bowl until smooth; drizzle over cinnamon rolls and serve.
Per Serving: Calories 163; Fat 9.44g; Sodium 20mg; Carbs 19.91g; Fibre 1.1g; Sugar 15.47g; Protein 0.93g

Oil-Free Fried Bacon

Prep Time: 5 minutes | **Cook Time:** 10 minutes | **Serves:** 4

8 bacon strips

1. Preheat the air fryer to 200°C. 2. Place the bacon strips in the air fryer basket in a single layer. Cook them for 10 minutes, turning halfway through. 3. Remove them from the air fryer after cooking, and place on a paper towel to absorb excess grease. 4. Serve warm.
Per Serving: Calories 212; Fat 20.42g; Sodium 244mg; Carbs 0.43g; Fibre 0g; Sugar 0.43g; Protein 6.52g

Simple Cherry Tarts

Prep time: 15 minutes| **Cook time:** 20 minutes| **Serves:** 6

For the tarts
2 refrigerated pie crusts
80ml cherry preserves
1 teaspoon cornflour
Cooking oil
For the frosting
118ml vanilla yoghurt
28g cream cheese
1 teaspoon stevia
Rainbow sprinkles

To make the tarts 1. Place the pie crusts on a flat surface. Cut each pie crust into 3 rectangles with a knife or pizza cutter for a total of 6 (I discard the unused dough left from slicing the edges). 2. Combine the cherry preserves and cornflour in a small bowl and mix well. 3. Scoop 1 tablespoon of the preserved mixture onto the top half of each piece of pie crust. 4. Fold up the bottom of each piece to close the tart. Using the back of a fork, press along the edges of each tart to seal. 5. Spray the breakfast tarts with cooking oil and place them in the air fryer. I do not recommend stacking the breakfast tarts as they will stick together if stacked. You may need to prepare them in 2 batches. Cook the breakfast tarts at 375°F/ 190°C for 10 minutes. 6. Allow the breakfast tarts to cool fully before removing them from the air fryer. Repeat the steps for the remaining breakfast tarts.
To make the frosting: in a small bowl, combine the yoghurt, cream cheese, and stevia. Mix well.
Spread the breakfast tarts with frosting and top with sprinkles, and serve.
Per Serving: Calories 368; Fat 20.6g; Sodium 346mg; Carbs 43g; Fibre 1g; Sugar 3g; Protein 3.7g

Grilled Ham and Cheese

Prep time: 5 minutes| **Cook time:** 10 minutes| **Serves:** 2

1 teaspoon butter
4 slices bread
4 slices smoked country ham
4 slices Cheddar cheese
4 thick slices tomato

1. Spread ½ teaspoon of butter onto 1 side of 2 slices of bread. Each sandwich will have 1 slice of bread with butter and 1 slice without. 2. Assemble each sandwich by layering 2 slices of ham, 2 slices of cheese, and 2 slices of tomato on the unbuttered pieces of bread. Then top with the other bread slices, buttered side up. 3. Place the sandwiches in the air fryer buttered-side down. Cook the sandwich at 370°F/ 185°C for 4 minutes. 4. Open the air fryer. Flip the grilled cheese sandwiches. Cook for an additional 4 minutes. 5. Cool before serving. Cut each sandwich in half and enjoy.
Per Serving: Calories 403; Fat 23.8g; Sodium 1162mg; Carbs 22g; Fibre 1.4g; Sugar 3.2g; Protein 25g

Tasty Hash Browns

Prep time: 15 minutes| **Cook time:** 20 minutes| **Serves:** 4

4 russet potatoes
1 teaspoon paprika
Salt
Pepper
Cooking oil

1. Peel the potatoes using a vegetable peeler. Using a cheese grater, shred the potatoes. If your grater has different-sized holes, use the area of the tool with the largest holes. 2. Place the shredded russet potatoes in a large bowl of cold water. Let sit for 5 minutes. Cold water helps remove excess starch from the potatoes. Stir to help dissolve the starch. 3. Drain the potatoes and dry them with paper towels or napkins. Make sure the potatoes are completely dry. Season the potatoes with the paprika and salt and pepper. 4. Spray the potatoes with cooking oil and transfer them to the air fryer. Cook the potatoes at 370°F/ 185°C for 20 minutes, shaking the basket every 5 minutes (a total of 4 times). Cool before serving.
Per Serving: Calories 185; Fat 1.5g; Sodium 303mg; Carbs 40g; Fibre 3g; Sugar 2g; Protein 4.9g

Cheese and Bacon Muffins

Prep time: 5 minutes| **Cook time:** 10 minutes| **Serves:** 4

4 muffins
8 slices Canadian bacon
4 slices cheese
Cooking oil

1. Split each muffin. Assemble the breakfast sandwiches by layering 2 slices of Canadian bacon and 1 slice of cheese onto each muffin bottom. Top the cheese slice with the other half of the muffin. 2. Place the sandwiches in the air fryer. Spray the top of each with cooking oil. Cook at 370°F/ 185°C for 4 minutes. 3. Open the air fryer and flip the sandwiches. Cook for an additional 4 minutes. Cool before serving.
Per Serving: Calories 289; Fat 10g; Sodium 1177mg; Carbs 29g; Fibre 2.6g; Sugar 3.9g; Protein 22g

Vanilla Strawberry Pastry

Prep Time: 30 minutes | **Cook Time:** 15 minutes | **Serves:** 8

1 (375g) package refrigerated piecrust
240g strawberry jam
1 large egg, whisked
60g icing sugar
2 tablespoons whole milk
½ teaspoon vanilla extract

1. Preheat the air fryer to 160°C. Cut parchment paper to fit the air fryer basket. 2. Lightly flour the work surface, and lay piecrusts out flat. 3. Cut each piecrust round into six 10 cm × 8 cm rectangles, reserving excess dough; form the remaining dough into a ball, then roll out and cut four additional 10 cm × 8 cm rectangles, bringing the total to sixteen. 4. Spread 15g jam on a pastry rectangle, leaving a 2cm border around the edges. Top with a second pastry rectangle and use a fork to gently press all four edges together. Do the same with the remaining jam and pastry. 5. Brush tops of each pastry with egg, and cut an X in the centre of each to prevent excess steam from building up. 6. Place pastries in the air fryer basket, cook them for 12 minutes; when the time is up, carefully flip and cook for an additional 3 minutes until each side is golden brown. 6. Let cool for 10 minutes. 7. Whisk the icing sugar, milk, and vanilla in a small bowl. 8. Brush each pastry with glaze, then place in the refrigerator 5 minutes to set before serving.
Per Serving: Calories 200; Fat 3.91g; Sodium 260mg; Carbs 36.14g; Fibre 1.4g; Sugar 7.58g; Protein 4.34g

Simple Bagels

Prep Time: 10 minutes | **Cook Time:** 10 minutes | **Serves:** 4

125g self-rising flour
245g plain full-fat Greek yogurt
2 tablespoons granulated sugar
1 large egg, whisked

1. Preheat the air fryer to 160°C. 2. In a large bowl, mix the flour, yogurt, and sugar in a large bowl until a ball of dough forms. 3. Lightly flour the work surface, turn dough out onto it. 4. Knead dough for 3 minutes, then form into a smooth ball. 5. Cut dough into four sections. Roll each piece into an 20cm rope, then shape into a circular bagel shape. Brush top and bottom of each bagel with egg. 6. Place them in the air fryer basket, and cook for 10 minutes, turning halfway through cooking time to ensure even browning. 7. Let cool for 5 minutes before serving.
Per Serving: Calories 180; Fat 2.37g; Sodium 430mg; Carbs 31.27g; Fibre 0.8g; Sugar 8.02g; Protein 7.64g

Golden Mini Potatoes

Prep Time: 5 minutes | **Cook Time:** 22 minutes | **Serves:** 4

1.4L water
455g baby Dutch yellow potatoes, quartered
2 tablespoons olive oil
½ teaspoon garlic powder
¾ teaspoon seasoned salt
¼ teaspoon salt
½ teaspoon ground black pepper

1. Boil the water in the medium saucepan over medium-high heat; add potatoes and boil for 10 minutes until fork-tender, then drain and gently pat dry. 2. Preheat the air fryer to 200°C. 3. Drizzle oil over potatoes, then sprinkle them with garlic powder, seasoned salt, salt, and pepper. 4. Place potatoes in the air fryer basket and cook for 12 minutes until golden brown and the edges are crisp. 5. Serve warm.
Per Serving: Calories 151; Fat 6.87g; Sodium 596mg; Carbs 20.63g; Fibre 2.6g; Sugar 1.18g; Protein 2.47g

Vegetable and Side Recipes

Potatoes Au Gratin

Prep Time: 15 minutes | **Cook Time:** 20 minutes | **Serves:** 4

120ml half-and-half
2 large eggs
1 tablespoon gluten-free plain flour
1 teaspoon salt
1 teaspoon ground black pepper
1 teaspoon smoked paprika
2 medium russet potatoes, scrubbed and thinly sliced
245g diced cooked ham
50g grated Gruyère cheese
1 tablespoon butter, melted
1 tablespoon grated Parmesan cheese
1 tablespoon gluten-free plain panko bread crumbs
1 tablespoon fresh thyme leaves

1. Whisk together half-and-half, eggs, flour, salt, pepper, and smoked paprika in a bowl. 2. Coat the potatoes with the egg mixture completely. 3. Preheat the air fryer to 190°C. Lightly grease a 17 cm round cake pan with preferred cooking oil. 4. Evenly distribute half of potato slices in the pan. Pour half of egg mixture over potatoes. Layer half of ham and Gruyère cheese on top. Do the same with remaining potato, egg mixture, ham, and Gruyère. 5. Mix the butter, Parmesan cheese, bread crumbs, and thyme leaves in a small bowl, and distribute over casserole. Cover the pan with aluminum foil. 6. Place the pan in air fryer basket, and cook the food for 15 minutes; remove the foil and cook for 5 minutes more. 7. Let the food rest 10 minutes after cooking. Serve warm.
Per Serving: Calories 306; Fat 10.05g; Sodium 1013mg; Carbs 41.73g; Fibre 3g; Sugar 2.87g; Protein 13.37g

Insalata Caprese

Prep Time: 5 minutes | **Cook Time:** 15 minutes | **Serves:** 2

100g grape tomatoes (approximately 16)
2 teaspoons olive oil, divided
¼ teaspoon salt
1 (200g) ball mozzarella cheese, sliced
1 tablespoon balsamic vinegar
1 tablespoon chopped fresh basil
¼ teaspoon ground black pepper

1. Preheat the air fryer to 175°C. 2. Toss the tomatoes with 1 teaspoon olive oil and salt. 3. Transfer the tomatoes to the air fryer basket, and cook for 15 minutes, shaking the basket every 5 minutes to cook evenly. 4. Apportion the mozzarella between two serving plates, top with the blistered tomatoes. Drizzle remaining oil and balsamic vinegar over tomatoes. Garnish with basil and black pepper. 5. Enjoy.
Per Serving: Calories 214; Fat 4.53g; Sodium 864mg; Carbs 7.19g; Fibre 2.2g; Sugar 4.42g; Protein 36.11g

Artichoke Hearts

Prep Time: 15 minutes | **Cook Time:** 8 minutes | **Serves:** 4

12 whole artichoke hearts packed in water, drained
60g plain flour
1 egg
35g panko bread crumbs
1 teaspoon Italian seasoning
Cooking oil spray

1. Squeeze any excess water from the artichoke hearts and pat them dry with paper towels to dry. 2. Place the flour in a small bowl, and beat the egg in the second bowl, then stir the panko and Italian seasoning in the third bowl. 3. Dip the artichoke hearts into the flour, then into the egg, and finally into the panko mixture until coated. 4. Spray the air fryer basket with cooking oil, and then arrange the coated artichoke hearts in the basket. 5. Cook the coated artichoke hearts in the air fryer at 190°C for 8 minutes on Air Fry mode, flipping them halfway through. 6. When the cooking is complete, the artichoke hearts should be deep golden brown and crisp. Let them cool for 5 minutes before serving.
Per Serving: Calories 273; Fat 2.52g; Sodium 298mg; Carbs 56.88g; Fibre 31.6g; Sugar 3.89g; Protein 13.69g

Lemon Broccoli

Prep Time: 10 minutes | **Cook Time:** 15 minutes | **Serves:** 4

1 large head broccoli, rinsed and patted dry
2 teaspoons extra-virgin olive oil
1 tablespoon freshly squeezed lemon juice
Olive oil spray

1. Preheat the air fryer to 200°C on Air Roast mode. Spray the air fryer basket with olive oil. 2. Cut off the broccoli florets and separate them. You can peel the stems and cut them into 2-cm chunks. 3. Coat the broccoli florets with the olive, and lemon juice in a large bowl. 4. Place half of the broccoli in the basket, and Air Roast them at 200°C for 15 minutes, tossing them every 5 minutes. You can cook them in batches. 5. Serve the broccoli on a bowl, and enjoy.
Per Serving: Calories 32; Fat 2.24g; Sodium 32mg; Carbs 2.77g; Fibre 1g; Sugar 0.74g; Protein 1.09g

Roasted Courgette and Red Peppers

Prep time: 5 minutes| **Cook time:** 15 minutes| **Serves:** 6

2 medium courgette, cubed
1 red pepper, diced
2 garlic cloves, sliced
2 tablespoons olive oil
½ teaspoon salt

1. Preheat the air fryer to 380°F/ 195°C. 2. Mix together the courgette, red pepper, and garlic with the olive oil and salt in a large bowl. 3. Transfer the mixture into the air fryer basket and roast for 7 minutes. Shake or stir, then roast for 7 to 8 minutes more.
Per Serving: Calories 55; Fat 4.8g; Sodium 200mg; Carbs 3g; Fibre 0.8g; Sugar 2g; Protein 1g

Parmesan Sweet Potatoes with Rosemary

Prep time: 10 minutes| **Cook time:** 18 minutes| **Serves:** 4

2 large sweet potatoes, peeled and cubed
60ml olive oil
1 teaspoon dried rosemary
½ teaspoon salt
2 tablespoons shredded Parmesan

1. Preheat the air fryer to 360°F/ 180°C. 2. Drizzle olive oil over the sweet potatoes in a large bowl, and season with salt and rosemary. 3. Then, transfer the sweet potatoes into the air fryer basket and roast for 10 minutes. Stir the sweet potatoes and sprinkle the Parmesan over the top. Continue roasting for 8 minutes more. 4. Serve hot and enjoy.
Per Serving: Calories 211; Fat 13.8g; Sodium 352mg; Carbs 19.8g; Fibre 3.1g; Sugar 5.9g; Protein 2.8g

Citrusy Roasted Brussels Sprouts

Prep time: 5 minutes| **Cook time:** 10 minutes| **Serves:** 4

1 pound Brussels sprouts, quartered
2 garlic cloves, minced
2 tablespoons olive oil
½ teaspoon salt
1 orange, cut into rings

1. Preheat the air fryer to 360°F/ 180°C. 2. Mix the quartered Brussels sprouts, garlic, olive oil, and salt in a large bowl until the Brussels sprouts are tossed well. 3. Pour the Brussels sprouts into the air fryer, lay the orange slices on top of them, and roast for 10 minutes. 4. Remove from the air fryer and set the orange slices aside. Toss the Brussels sprouts before serving.
Per Serving: Calories 128; Fat 7.2g; Sodium 320mg; Carbs 15g; Fibre 5.1g; Sugar 5.5g; Protein 4.3g

Crispy Crusted Artichoke Hearts

Prep time: 10 minutes| **Cook time:** 15 minutes| **Serves:** 2

1 (425g) can artichoke hearts in water, drained
1 egg
1 tablespoon water
30g whole wheat breadcrumbs
¼ teaspoon salt
¼ teaspoon paprika
½ lemon

1. Preheat the air fryer to 380°F/ 195°C. 2. Beat the egg and water in a medium shallow bowl until frothy. 3. In a separate medium shallow bowl, mix together the bread crumbs, salt, and paprika. 4. Dip each artichoke heart into the egg mixture, then into the bread crumb mixture, coating the outside with the crumbs. Place the artichoke hearts in a single layer of the air fryer basket. 5. Fry the artichoke hearts for 15 minutes. 6. Then remove the artichokes from the air fryer, and squeeze fresh lemon juice over the top before serving.
Per Serving: Calories 188; Fat 3.2g; Sodium 621mg; Carbs 33.2g; Fibre 12.2g; Sugar 3.4g; Protein 11.6g

Flavourful Green Tomatoes

Prep Time: 15 minutes | **Cook Time:** 30 minutes | **Serves:** 4

60g plain flour
2 eggs
60g polenta
55g panko bread crumbs
1 teaspoon garlic powder
Salt
Freshly ground black pepper
2 green tomatoes, cut into 1-cm-thick rounds
Cooking oil spray

1. Preheat the air fryer to 200°C on Air Fry mode. Spray the air fryer basket with cooking oil. 2. Beat the eggs in a small bowl, place the flour in the second bowl, and mix the polenta, panko, garlic powder, salt, and pepper in the third bowl. 3. Dip each tomato slice into the flour, then into the egg, and finally into the polenta mixture to coat. Transfer the coated tomato slices to the basket in a single layer (do not stack them), and spray them with the cooking oil. 4. Air Fry them for 10 minutes until crisp, flipping halfway through. You can cook them in batches as need. 5. Serve and enjoy.
Per Serving: Calories 199; Fat 3.99g; Sodium 102mg; Carbs 33.55g; Fibre 2.1g; Sugar 3.17g; Protein 7.03g

Parmesan Aubergine

Prep Time: 15 minutes | **Cook Time:** 30 minutes | **Serves:** 4

1 medium aubergine, peeled and cut into 1-cm-thick rounds
1 teaspoon salt, plus more for seasoning
60g plain flour
2 eggs
90g Italian bread crumbs
2 tablespoons grated Parmesan cheese
Freshly ground black pepper
Cooking oil spray
180g marinara sauce
40g shredded Parmesan cheese, divided
45g shredded mozzarella cheese, divided

1. Preheat the air fryer to 200°C on Air Fry mode. Spray the air fryer basket with cooking oil. 2. Pat the aubergine dry with paper towels. 3. Beat the egg in a shallow bowl, add the flour to the second bowl, and mix the bread crumbs, Parmesan cheese, salt and pepper in the third bowl. 4. Dip each aubergine round in the flour, then in the eggs, and finally in the bread crumbs. 5. Working in batches, place the coated aubergine rounds in the basket (do not stack them), and spray them with the cooking oil. 6. Air Fry them for 10 minutes; after 7 minutes of cooking time, top each aubergine round with 1 teaspoon of marinara sauce, ½ tablespoon each of shredded Parmesan and mozzarella cheese, then resume cooking. 7. Do the same with the remaining aubergine rounds. 8. When done, serve immediately.
Per Serving: Calories 258; Fat 8.73g; Sodium 1038mg; Carbs 29.87g; Fibre 5.8g; Sugar 8.2g; Protein 15.72g

Four Cheese Macaroni

Prep Time: 15 minutes | **Cook Time:** 20 minutes | **Serves:** 4

3 tablespoons butter, divided
1 large sweet yellow onion, peeled and diced
1 tablespoon gluten-free plain flour
100g cream cheese, room temperature
60g shredded Swiss cheese
25g shredded sharp Cheddar cheese
25g grated Parmesan cheese
60ml whole milk
220g dry gluten-free elbow macaroni, cooked according to package instructions, drained
30g gluten-free bread crumbs

1. Heat 2 tablespoons of butter in the skillet over medium-high heat for 30 seconds; add onion and cook for 3 minutes until onions are translucent. 2. Whisk in flour until sauce thickens. 3. Stir in cream cheese, Swiss cheese, Cheddar cheese, Parmesan cheese, and milk to skillet; add the pasta and toss. 4. Preheat air fryer to 190°C. 5. In a small bowl, mix the bread crumbs and remaining butter. 6. Spoon the pasta mixture into a 17 cm round cake barrel, which is lightly greased with preferred cooking oil. Top with buttered bread crumbs. 7. Place the pan in air fryer basket, and cook the food for 15 minutes. 8. Let the food rest for 10 minutes after cooking, then serve warm.
Per Serving: Calories 280; Fat 22.14g; Sodium 364mg; Carbs 14.12g; Fibre 0.9g; Sugar 5.28g; Protein 8g

Watermelon Salad

Prep Time: 10 minutes | **Cook Time:** 4 minutes | **Serves:** 4

610g (1-cm cubes) watermelon
½ medium red onion, peeled and sliced into half-moons
4 teaspoons olive oil, divided
½ teaspoon salt
¼ teaspoon ground black pepper
60g rocket
1 teaspoon balsamic vinegar
1 teaspoon honey
2 tablespoons crumbled goat cheese
1 tablespoon chopped fresh mint

1. Preheat air fryer at 190°C for 3 minutes. 2. Toss watermelon and onion with 2 teaspoons of olive oil, and season them with salt and pepper. 3. Add the watermelon mixture to air fryer basket, cook them for 4 minutes, tossing them halfway through. 4. Coat the rocket with the remaining olive oil, balsamic vinegar, and honey. 5. Add watermelon and onion to rocket mixture, and garnish with goat cheese and mint. Serve warm.
Per Serving: Calories 121; Fat 6.46g; Sodium 421mg; Carbs 15.15g; Fibre 1g; Sugar 12.37g; Protein 2.69g

Lemony Roasted Green Beans

Prep time: 5 minutes| **Cook time:** 10 minutes| **Serves:** 6

450g fresh green beans, trimmed
½ red onion, sliced
2 tablespoons olive oil
½ teaspoon salt
¼ teaspoon black pepper
1 tablespoon lemon juice
Lemon wedges, for serving

1. Preheat the air fryer to 360°F/ 180°C. Toss the green beans, onion, olive oil, salt, pepper, and lemon juice in a large bowl until combined. 2. Pour the mixture into the air fryer and roast for 5 minutes. Stir well and roast for 5 minutes more. 3. Serve with lemon wedges.
Per Serving: Calories 62; Fat 4.9g; Sodium 196mg; Carbs 4.7g; Fibre 1.7g; Sugar 1.2g; Protein 1g

Honey Carrots and Walnuts

Prep time: 5 minutes| **Cook time:** 12 minutes| **Serves:** 6

450g baby carrots
2 tablespoons olive oil
80ml raw honey
¼ teaspoon ground cinnamon
30g black walnuts, chopped

1. Preheat the air fryer to 360°F/ 180°C. 2. Mix the baby carrots, olive oil, honey, and cinnamon in a large bowl until well coated. 3. Transfer into the air fryer and then roast for 6 minutes. Shake the basket, sprinkle with the walnuts, and continue roasting for 6 minutes or more. 4. Transfer the carrots onto a serving plate.
Per Serving: Calories 142; Fat 7.7g; Sodium 45mg; Carbs 18.5g; Fibre 2.7g; Sugar 14.3g; Protein 1.9g

Roasted Asparagus and Grape Tomatoes

Prep time: 5 minutes| **Cook time:** 12 minutes| **Serves:** 6

300g grape tomatoes
1 bunch asparagus, trimmed
2 tablespoons olive oil
3 garlic cloves, minced
½ teaspoon kosher salt

1. Preheat the air fryer to 380°F/ 195°C. 2. In a large bowl, combine the grape tomatoes, asparagus, olive oil, garlic cloves, and kosher salt, tossing until the vegetables are well coated with oil. 3. Pour the vegetable mixture into the air fryer basket and spread into a single layer, then roast for 12 minutes.
Per Serving: Calories 77; Fat 4.6g; Sodium 195mg; Carbs 9.7g; Fibre 0.6g; Sugar 7.9g; Protein 0.5g

Greek Buffalo Cauliflower

Prep Time: 15 minutes | **Cook Time:** 7 minutes | **Serves:** 6

1 large head cauliflower, rinsed and separated into small florets
1 tablespoon extra-virgin olive oil
½ teaspoon garlic powder
Cooking oil spray
80ml hot wing sauce
150g nonfat Greek yogurt
60ml buttermilk
½ teaspoon hot sauce (such as Frank's Red-hot or Tabasco)
1 celery stalk, chopped
2 tablespoons crumbled blue cheese

1. Preheat the air fryer to 190°C on Air Fry mode. Spray the air fryer basket with cooking oil. 2. Coat the cauliflower florets with the olive oil and garlic powder. 3. Add half of the coated cauliflower florets to the basket, and Air Fry them for 7 minutes. 4. After 3 minutes, remove the basket and shake the cauliflower. Reinsert the basket to resume cooking. After 2 minutes, check the cauliflower. It is done when it is browned. If not, resume cooking. 5. Do the same with the remaining cauliflower florets. 6. Whisk the yogurt, buttermilk, celery, hot sauce, and blue cheese in a small bowl. 7. After cooking, toss the cauliflower florets with the hot wing sauce in the serving bowl, then drizzle the yogurt sauce over them. Enjoy.
Per Serving: Calories 59; Fat 2.75g; Sodium 167mg; Carbs 4.41g; Fibre 1g; Sugar 2.52g; Protein 4.77g

Spiced Kale Chips

Prep Time: 7 minutes | **Cook Time:** 5 minutes | **Serves:** 4

1 tablespoon chili powder
1 tablespoon nacho cheese powder
1 teaspoon ground cumin
½ teaspoon dried oregano
½ teaspoon garlic powder
¼ teaspoon onion powder
⅛ teaspoon paprika
85g loosely packed kale, stemmed and chopped into chip-size pieces
2 tablespoons extra-virgin olive oil
Cooking oil spray

1. Preheat the air fryer to 190°C on Bake mode. Spray the air fryer basket with cooking oil. 2. Mix the chili powder, nacho cheese powder, cumin, oregano, garlic powder, onion powder, and paprika in a small bowl. 3. Coat the kale with olive oil and the seasoning in a medium bowl. 4. Transfer the kale to the basket, and Air Fry them for 5 minutes until crisp. 5. After 2 minutes of cooking, toss the kale and resume cooking. 6. Serve and enjoy.
Per Serving: Calories 59; Fat 4.92g; Sodium 130mg; Carbs 3.51g; Fibre 1.5g; Sugar 0.58g; Protein 1.29g

Brussels Sprouts with Honey-Sriracha Sauce

Prep Time: 10 minutes | **Cook Time:** 18 minutes | **Serves:** 4

1 teaspoon plus 1 tablespoon extra-virgin olive oil, divided
2 teaspoons minced garlic
2 tablespoons honey
1 tablespoon sugar
2 tablespoons freshly squeezed lemon juice
2 tablespoons rice vinegar
2 tablespoons sriracha
455g Brussels sprouts, stems trimmed and any tough leaves removed, rinsed, halved lengthwise, and dried
½ teaspoon salt
Cooking oil spray

1. Add 1 teaspoon of olive oil, the garlic, honey, sugar, lemon juice, vinegar, and sriracha to a small saucepan, and cook them over low heat for 2 to 3 minutes until slightly thickened. Remove the pan from the heat, cover it, and set aside. 2. Toss the Brussels sprouts with the remaining olive oil and salt in a small bowl. 3. Preheat the air fryer to 200°C on Air Fry mode. 4. Spray the air fryer basket with cooking oil, and add the Brussels sprouts to it. 5. Air Fry the Brussels sprouts for 15 minutes until the sprout are tender, and the leaves are crispy and light brown, tossing them halfway through. 6. Place the sprouts in a medium serving bowl and drizzle the sauce over the top. Toss to coat, and enjoy immediately.
Per Serving: Calories 11; Fat 1.99g; Sodium 393mg; Carbs 22.46g; Fibre 4.5g; Sugar 13.66g; Protein 4.12g

Savory Sweet Potatoes

Prep Time: 10 minutes | **Cook Time:** 25 minutes | **Serves:** 4

Cooking oil spray
2 sweet potatoes, peeled and cut into 2cm cubes
1 tablespoon extra-virgin olive oil
Pinch salt
Freshly ground black pepper
½ teaspoon dried thyme
½ teaspoon dried marjoram
30 g grated Parmesan cheese

1. Preheat the air fryer to 165°C on Air Roast mode. Spray the air fryer basket with cooking oil. 2. Coat the sweet potato cubes with olive oil, and then toss them with the thyme, marjoram, salt, and pepper. 3. Transfer the sweet potato cubes to the basket, and Air Roast them for 25 minutes until tender, shaking the basket every 10 minutes. 4. Serve hot.
Per Serving: Calories 106; Fat 4.41g; Sodium 217mg; Carbs 14.03g; Fibre 2g; Sugar 2.72g; Protein 2.83g

Bacon and Cheese Rotini

Prep Time: 15 minutes | **Cook Time:** 20 minutes | **Serves:** 4

3 tablespoons butter, divided
1 tablespoon gluten-free plain flour
50g cream cheese, room temperature
50g shredded sharp Cheddar cheese
55g shredded mozzarella cheese
60g heavy cream
225g dry gluten-free rotini, cooked according to package instructions, drained
4 pieces cooked bacon, crumbled
30g gluten-free bread crumbs

1. Preheat the air fryer to 190°C. 2. Heat 2 tablespoons of butter in the skillet over medium-high heat for 30 seconds, then whisk in flour until the sauce thickens. 3. Add cream cheese, Cheddar cheese, mozzarella cheese, and heavy cream, and cook them for 2 minutes until creamy; add pasta and bacon and toss to coat. 4. Place the remaining butter in a microwave-safe bowl, and cook in microwave for 10 seconds until melted, then min in the bread crumbs. 5. Lightly grease a suitable cake barrel with preferred cooking oil. Spoon the pasta mixture in this cake barrel, and top with buttered bread crumbs. 6. Bake the food in the air fryer for 15 minutes. 7. Let the food rest for 10 minutes after baking, and then, serve warm.
Per Serving: Calories 504; Fat 27.17g; Sodium 870mg; Carbs 51.73g; Fibre 2.3g; Sugar 3.19g; Protein 16.22g

Lime Peppers

Prep Time: 5 minutes | **Cook Time:** 9 minutes | **Serves:** 4

Cooking oil spray (sunflower, safflower, or refined coconut)
454g peppers, rinsed
1 tablespoon soy sauce
2 teaspoons freshly squeezed lime juice
2 large garlic cloves, pressed

1. Preheat the air fryer to 200°C on Air Roast mode. 2. Spray the air fryer basket with cooking oil, and place the peppers in the basket, and then spray them with oil. 3. Roast the peppers at 200°C for 9 minutes, tossing the peppers and spraying them more oil every 3 minutes. 4. Mix the soy sauce, lime juice, and garlic in a bowl. 5. When cooked, several of the peppers should have lots of nice browned spots on them. 6. Place the roasted peppers in the bowl with the sauce, and evenly coat them with the sauce before serving.
Per Serving: Calories 60; Fat 1.02g; Sodium 68mg; Carbs 12.44g; Fibre 1.8g; Sugar 6.61g; Protein 2.66g

Roasted Corn

Prep Time: 10 minutes | **Cook Time:** 6 minutes | **Serves:** 4

4 ears corn, shucked and halved crosswise
1 tablespoon extra-virgin olive oil
Salt
Freshly ground black pepper
Cooking oil spray

1. Preheat the air fryer to 200°C on Air Roast mode. Spray the air fryer basket with cooking oil. 2. Coat the corn with the olive oil, and season them with salt and pepper. 3. Place the corn in the basket, and Air Roast them for 6 minutes. 4. Let the corn cool for 5 minutes after cooking. 5. Serve and enjoy.
Per Serving: Calories 86; Fat 3.61g; Sodium 80mg; Carbs 13.67g; Fibre 1.5g; Sugar 4.57g; Protein 2.4g

Glazed Carrots with Sweet Potatoes

Prep Time: 5 minutes | **Cook Time:** 25 minutes | **Serves:** 4

2 large carrots, cut into 2cm chunks
1 medium sweet potato, peeled and cut into 2cm cubes
55g chopped onion
2 garlic cloves, minced
2 tablespoons honey
1 tablespoon freshly squeezed orange juice
2 teaspoons butter, melted

1. Preheat the air fryer to 200°C on Air Roast mode. 2. Toss the all of the ingredients in a suitable baking pan. 3. Air Roast the food in the air fryer for 25 minutes; after 15 minutes of cooking time, toss the vegetables. 4. Serve immediately after cooking.
Per Serving: Calories 115; Fat 2.09g; Sodium 30mg; Carbs 23.67g; Fibre 2.5g; Sugar 11.69g; Protein 1.74g

Snack and Starter Recipes

Cheeses Dip

Prep Time: 5 minutes | **Cook Time:** 12 minutes | **Serves:** 8

200g cream cheese, softened
110g mayonnaise
60g sour cream
50g shredded sharp Cheddar cheese
30g shredded Monterey jack cheese

1. Combine all the ingredients in a large bowl. 2. Scoop the mixture into an ungreased nonstick baking dish, and then place the baking dish in the air fryer basket. 3. Cook the mixture at 190°C for 12 minutes until the tops are browned and bubbling. 4. Serve warm.
Per Serving: Calories 186; Fat 17.28g; Sodium 316mg; Carbs 2.14g; Fibre 0.2g; Sugar 1.18g; Protein 5.89g

Cheddar Chicken Dip

Prep Time: 10 minutes | **Cook Time:** 12 minutes | **Serves:** 8

200g cream cheese, softened
280g chopped cooked chicken thighs
120ml buffalo sauce
100g shredded mild Cheddar cheese, divided

1. Combine the cream cheese, chicken, buffalo sauce, and 50g Cheddar in a large bowl. 2. Scoop the dip into an ungreased nonstick baking dish, and top them with the remaining Cheddar. 3. Place the dish in the air fryer basket, and cook the dip at 190°C for 12 minutes until the top are browned and bubbling. 4. Serve warm.
Per Serving: Calories 201; Fat 12.27g; Sodium 500mg; Carbs 9.8g; Fibre 0.2g; Sugar 7.93g; Protein 12.54g

Cheese Pepperoni Rolls

Prep Time: 5 minutes | **Cook Time:** 8 minutes | **Serves:** 6

280g shredded mozzarella cheese
50g cream cheese, softened
100g blanched finely ground almond flour
48 slices pepperoni
2 teaspoons Italian seasoning

1. Combine mozzarella, cream cheese, and flour in a microwave-safe bowl, and then microwave them on high for 90 seconds until cheese is melted. 2. Mix the melted mixture for 2 minutes until a dough forms. 3. Let the dough sit for 2 minutes, and then spread it out into a 30 cm × 10 cm rectangle on the parchment paper. 4. Line the dough with pepperoni, and evenly divide into four rows. Sprinkle the Italian seasoning over pepperoni evenly. 5. From the long end of the dough, roll up until a log is formed, then slice the log into 12 pieces. 6. Transfer the rolls to a suitable nonstick baking dish. 7. Cook the rolls in the air fryer at 190°C for 8 minutes until they are golden and firm. 8. Let the rolls cool for 10 minutes after cooking, then enjoy.
Per Serving: Calories 252; Fat 9.87g; Sodium 742mg; Carbs 18.43g; Fibre 1.5g; Sugar 1.19g; Protein 21.46g

Tasty Courgette Fries

Prep Time: 2 hours 10 minutes | **Cook Time:** 10 minutes | **Serves:** 8

2 medium courgettes, ends removed, quartered lengthwise, and sliced into 7-cm long fries
½ teaspoon salt
70g heavy whipping cream
50g blanched finely ground almond flour
75g grated Parmesan cheese
1 teaspoon Italian seasoning

1. Sprinkle the courgette slices with salt, and wrap in a kitchen towel to draw out excess moisture. Let them sit for 2 hours. 2. Add the cream to a medium bowl, and whisk the flour, Parmesan, and Italian seasoning in another medium bowl. 3. Dip the courgette slice in the cream, shaking off excess gently, and then coat the courgette slice with the flour mixture on both side. Do the same with the remaining courgette slices. 4. Place the courgette slices in the air fryer basket, and cook them in the air fryer at 200°C for 10 minutes until golden and crispy, turning them halfway through. 5. Let the courgette slices cool for 5 minutes after cooking, then enjoy.
Per Serving: Calories 97; Fat 4.53g; Sodium 343mg; Carbs 7.7g; Fibre 0.3g; Sugar 0.21g; Protein 3.66g

Fried Ranch Pickle Spears

Prep Time: 40 minutes | **Cook Time:** 10 minutes | **Serves:** 4

4 dill pickle spears, halved lengthwise
60ml ranch dressing
50g blanched finely ground almond flour
50g grated Parmesan cheese
2 tablespoons dry ranch seasoning

1. Wrap the spears and place in a kitchen towel for 30 minutes to soak up excess pickle juice. 2. Add the ranch dressing and pickle spears in a medium bowl. 3. Mix the flour, Parmesan, and dry ranch seasoning in another bowl. 4. Remove the spears from the ranch dressing and shake off excess, and coat with the flour mixture. 5. Place the spears in the air fryer basket, and cook them at 200°C for 10 minutes, turning the spears three times during cooking. 6. Serve warm.
Per Serving: Calories 190; Fat 10.42g; Sodium 952mg; Carbs 17.85g; Fibre 1.3g; Sugar 1.59g; Protein 5.73g

Bacon Mozzarella Sticks

Prep Time: 12 minutes | **Cook Time:** 12 minutes | **Serves:** 6

6 sticks mozzarella string cheese
6 slices bacon

1. Place mozzarella sticks on a medium plate, cover the plate, and freeze for 1 hour until frozen solid. 2. Wrap each mozzarella stick with one bacon piece, and secure them with a toothpick. Do the same with the sticks and bacon slices. 3. Cook the sticks in the air fryer at 200°C for 12 minutes until the bacon slices are crispy, turning the sticks halfway through. 4. Serve warm.
Per Serving: Calories 131; Fat 8.7g; Sodium 409mg; Carbs 1.17g; Fibre 0g; Sugar 1.06g; Protein 12.1g

Crispy Avocado Fries

Prep Time: 10 minutes | **Cook Time:** 6 minutes | **Serves:** 6

1 large egg
30g coconut flour
55g pork crackling, finely crushed
2 medium avocados, peeled, pitted, and sliced into ½ cm-thick fries

1. Whisk the egg in a medium bowl, add the coconut flour in the second bowl, and place the pork cracklings in the third bowl. 2. Dip the avocado slice into the whisked egg, then coat in coconut flour. Dip in egg once more, then press gently into pork cracklings to coat on both sides. 3. Do the same with the remaining avocado slices. 4. Place the coated avocado slices in the air fryer basket, and cook them in the air fryer at 200°C for 6 minutes until they are crispy on the outside and soft inside, turning them halfway through. 5. Let the avocado fries cool for a while after cooking, then enjoy.
Per Serving: Calories 159; Fat 12.29g; Sodium 22mg; Carbs 9.76g; Fibre 4.6g; Sugar 0.49g; Protein 4.38g

Hot Turkey Meatballs

Prep Time: 10 minutes | **Cook Time:** 15 minutes | **Serves:** 6

455g lean turkey mince
1 large egg, whisked
60ml sriracha hot chile sauce
½ teaspoon salt
½ teaspoon paprika
¼ teaspoon ground black pepper

1. Combine all ingredients in a large bowl. 2. Make the mixture into 18 meatballs, and place them in the air fryer basket. 3. Cook them in the air fryer at 190°C for 15 minutes until they are browned and have an internal temperature of at least 75°C. 4. Shake the basket three times during cooking. 5. Serve warm.
Per Serving: Calories 151; Fat 10.36g; Sodium 249mg; Carbs 0.64g; Fibre 0.2g; Sugar 0.31g; Protein 13.96g

Salami Cheese Roll-Ups

Prep Time: 5 minutes | **Cook Time:** 4 minutes | **Serves:** 4

110g cream cheese, broken into 16 equal pieces
16 (15g) deli slices Genoa salami

1. Place a cream cheese piece at the edge of a salami slice, and roll to close. Secure them with a toothpick. 2. Do the same with the remaining cream cheese pieces and salami. 3. Place the roll-ups in a suitable nonstick baking dish, and put the dish in the air fryer basket. 4. Cook the roll-ups in the air fryer at 175°C for 4 minutes until the salami slices are crispy. 5. Let them cool for 5 minutes after cooking, then serve.
Per Serving: Calories 97; Fat 9.23g; Sodium 186mg; Carbs 1.02g; Fibre 0g; Sugar 1g; Protein 2.76g

Garlic Crostini with Cheese

Prep time: 3 minutes| **Cook time:** 5 minutes| **Serves:** 4

1 whole-wheat baguette
60ml olive oil
2 garlic cloves, minced
110g goat cheese
2 tablespoons fresh basil, minced

1. Preheat the air fryer to 380°F/ 195°C. 2. Cut the baguette into ½-inch-thick slices. 3. In a small bowl, mix together the olive oil and garlic, then brush it over one side of each slice of bread. 4. Place the olive-oil-coated bread in a single layer in the air fryer basket and bake for 5 minutes. 5. Meanwhile, in a small bowl, mix together the goat cheese and basil. 6. Remove the toast from the air fryer, then spread a thin layer of the goat cheese mixture over the top of each piece and serve.
Per Serving: Calories 320; Fat 24g; Sodium 279mg; Carbs 14.8g; Fibre 0.7g; Sugar 1.4g; Protein 11.7g

Air-Fried Vegetable Spring Rolls

Prep time: 10 minutes| **Cook time:** 9 minutes| **Serves:** 16

4 teaspoons toasted sesame oil
6 medium garlic cloves, minced or pressed
1 tablespoon grated peeled fresh ginger
180g thinly sliced shiitake mushrooms
500g chopped green cabbage
170g grated carrot
½ teaspoon sea salt
16 rice paper wrappers
Gluten-free sweet and sour sauce, for serving (optional)
Thai sweet chilli sauce, for serving (optional)
Cooking oil spray

1. Set a wok or sauté pan over medium heat until hot. 2. Add the sesame oil, mushrooms, cabbage, garlic, ginger, salt, and carrot. Cook and stir for 3 to 4 minutes, or until the vegetables are lightly wilted. Then turn off the heat. 3. Unfold a rice paper gently under running water. Then lay it on a clean flat countertop. 4. In the middle of the rice paper, add ¼ cup of the cabbage filling. 5. Roll the softened wrapper to make a tiny burrito by folding the bottom up over the filling with the sides folded and the wrapper all the way up. 6. Repeat the steps to make enough spring roll as you want. Store any leftover filling in an air-tight container in a refrigerator for up to 1 week. 7. To preheat, set your air fryer to 390°F/ 200°C for about 3 minutes with a crisper plate inserted inside your air fryer basket in your air fryer. 8. Spray the crisper plate and the air fryer basket with cooking oil. 9. Arrange the spring rolls onto the prepared crisper plate, leaving a little room between them to avoid them from sticking to each other, and then spray the spring rolls with cooking oil. 10. Cook under the instruction of your air fryer at 390°F/ 200°C for 9 minutes. 11. When the spring rolls are cooked, they shall be crisped and lightly browned. Serve immediately or with your favourite sauce.
Per Serving: Calories 70; Fat 1.4g; Sodium 128mg; Carbs 13.4g; Fibre 1g; Sugar 1.3g; Protein 1.2g

Feta Courgette Roulades

Prep time: 10 minutes| **Cook time:** 10 minutes| **Serves:** 6

120g feta
1 garlic clove, minced
2 tablespoons fresh basil, minced
1 tablespoon capers, minced
⅛ teaspoon salt
⅛ teaspoon red pepper flakes
1 tablespoon lemon juice
2 medium courgettes
12 toothpicks

1. Preheat the air fryer to 360°F/ 180°C. (If using a grill attachment, make sure it is inside the air fryer during preheating.) 2. In a suitable bowl, combine the feta, garlic, basil, capers, salt, red pepper flakes, and lemon juice. 3. Slice the courgette into ⅛-inch strips lengthwise (each courgette should yield around 6 strips). 4. Spread 1 tablespoon of the cheese filling onto each slice of courgette, then roll it up and secure it with a toothpick through the middle. 5. Place the courgettes roulades into the air fryer basket in a single layer, making sure that they don't touch each other. 6. Bake or grill in the air fryer for 10 minutes. 7. Remove the courgettes roulades from the air fryer and gently remove the toothpicks before serving.
Per Serving: Calories 36; Fat 2.7g; Sodium 200mg; Carbs 1.2g; Fibre 0.1g; Sugar 0.6g; Protein 2g

Roasted Herbed Tomatoes and Olives

Prep time: 5 minutes| **Cook time:** 20 minutes| **Serves:** 6

480g cherry tomatoes
4 garlic cloves, roughly chopped
½ red onion, roughly chopped
135g black olives
130g green olives
1 tablespoon fresh basil, minced
1 tablespoon fresh oregano, minced
2 tablespoons olive oil
¼ to ½ teaspoon salt

1. Preheat the air fryer to 380°F/ 195°C. 2. In a large bowl, combine all of the ingredients and toss together so that the tomatoes and olives are coated well with the olive oil and herbs. 3. Pour the mixture into the air fryer basket and roast for 10 minutes. Stir the mixture well, then continue roasting for an additional 10 minutes. 4. Remove from the air fryer, transfer to a serving bowl, and enjoy.
Per Serving: Calories 80; Fat 6.8g; Sodium 273mg; Carbs 5g; Fibre 1.6g; Sugar 1.7g; Protein 1g

Simple Chips

Prep time: 35 minutes| **Cook time:** 30 minutes| **Serves:** 6

3 large russet potatoes, peeled and cut lengthwise into fry shapes
1 tablespoon canola oil
1 tablespoon extra-virgin olive oil
Salt
Freshly ground black pepper
Cooking oil spray
Fresh parsley, for garnish (optional)

1. Place the potatoes in a large bowl of cold water and let soak for at least 30 minutes, preferably 1 hour. Drain the potatoes and thoroughly dry them using a clean kitchen towel. 2. Insert the crisper plate into the basket of your air fryer. Preheat the unit by selecting AIR FRY, setting the temperature to 390°F/ 200°C, and setting the time to 3 minutes. 3. Spread the chips onto a baking sheet (optional: lined with parchment paper) and coat them with the canola oil and olive oil. Season with salt and pepper. 4. Once the unit is preheated, spray the crisper plate with cooking oil. Place half the chips into the basket. 5. Select AIR FRY, set the temperature to 390°F/ 200°C, and set the time to 15 minutes. 6. Cook for 10 minutes and then remove the basket and shake it so the chips at the bottom come up to the top. Reinsert the basket to resume cooking. 7. When the cooking is complete, transfer the chips to a plate. Repeat the cooking steps for the remaining chips. 8. When the second batch is complete, return all the chips to the basket and shake it. Air fry for 1 minute more so all the fries are hot before serving. Garnish with chopped parsley (if using).
Per Serving: Calories 175; Fat 3.5g; Sodium 29mg; Carbs 33.3g; Fibre 2.4g; Sugar 1.1g; Protein 4g

Cinnamon Apple Chips

Prep time: 5 minutes| **Cook time:** 7 to 8 hours| **Serves:** 4
4 medium apples, any type, cored and cut into ⅓-inch-thick slices (thin slices yield crunchy chips)
¼ teaspoon ground cinnamon
¼ teaspoon ground nutmeg

1. Place the apple slices in a large bowl. Sprinkle the cinnamon and nutmeg onto the apple slices and toss to coat. 2. Insert the crisper plate into the basket of your air fryer. Preheat the unit by selecting DEHYDRATE, setting the temperature to 135°F/ 55°C, and setting the time to 3 minutes. 3. Once the unit is preheated, place the apple chips into the basket. It is okay to stack them. 4. Select DEHYDRATE, set the temperature to 135°F/ 55°C, and set the time to 7 or 8 hours. Select START/STOP to begin. 5. When the cooking is complete, cool the apple chips. Serve or store at room temperature in an air-tight container for up to 1 week.
Per Serving: Calories 96; Fat 0.4g; Sodium 2mg; Carbs 25.4g; Fibre 4.5g; Sugar 19g; Protein 0.5g

Cheese Cauliflower Buns

Prep Time: 15 minutes | **Cook Time:** 12 minutes | **Serves:** 8

1 (300g) steamer bag cauliflower, cooked according to package instructions
55g shredded mozzarella cheese
25g shredded mild Cheddar cheese
25g blanched finely ground almond flour
1 large egg
½ teaspoon salt

1. Place the cooked and cooled cauliflower in a food processor after using the kitchen towel to wring out excess moisture. 2. Add the mozzarella, Cheddar, flour, egg, and salt to the food processor, and pulse them with the cauliflower 20 times until combined. 3. Divide the mixture into 8 piles, and press each pile into a flat bun shape, about 1-cm thick (you should wet your hands to prevent sticking). 4. Line the air fryer basket with parchment paper, and place the formed dough on it. 5. Cook the dough in the air fryer at 175°C for 12 minutes, turning them halfway through. 6. Let the buns cool for 10 minutes after cooking, then serve warm.
Per Serving: Calories 49; Fat 1.14g; Sodium 252mg; Carbs 5.41g; Fibre 1.2g; Sugar 1.27g; Protein 4.69g

Mini Spinach Meatballs

Prep Time: 10 minutes | **Cook Time:** 10 minutes | **Serves:** 9

240g fresh spinach leaves
20g peeled and diced red onion
120g crumbled feta cheese
454g lean turkey mince
½ teaspoon salt
½ teaspoon ground cumin
¼ teaspoon ground black pepper

1. Place spinach, onion, and feta in a food processor, and pulse them 10 times until spinach is chopped. Then transfer the mixture to a large bowl. 2. Add the turkey, salt, cumin, and pepper to the bowl, mix them with the spinach mixture well. 3. Make the mixture into 36 meatballs. 4. Place the meatballs in the air fryer basket, and cook them at 175°C for 10 minutes until they are browned and have an internal temperature of at least 75°C, shaking the basket twice during cooking. 5. Serve warm.
Per Serving: Calories 115; Fat 8.14g; Sodium 236mg; Carbs 0.86g; Fibre 0.2g; Sugar 0.49g; Protein 9.86g

Sweet Beef Jerky

Prep Time: 2 hours | **Cook Time:** 4 hours | **Serves:** 6

454g eye of ground beef, fat trimmed, sliced into ½ cm-thick strips
60ml soy sauce
2 tablespoons sriracha hot chili sauce
½ teaspoon ground black pepper
2 tablespoons granular brown sweetener

1. Place the beef, soy sauce, sriracha, pepper, and sweetener in a large sealable bowl, then stir them to combine ingredients and coat steak. 2. Cover the bowl and place in refrigerator to marinate for at least 2 hours up to overnight. 3. When marinated, remove the beef strips from the marinade, and pat them dry, then, place them in the air fryer basket. 4. Cook the beef strips at 80°C for 4 hours until chewy and dark brown. 5. You can store the beef strips in an airtight container in a cool, dry place for up to 2 weeks.
Per Serving: Calories 147; Fat 7.23g; Sodium 307mg; Carbs 3.21g; Fibre 0.3g; Sugar 2.18g; Protein 17.65g

Mayonnaise Eggs

Prep Time: 10 minutes | **Cook Time:** 25 minutes | **Serves:** 6

7 large eggs, divided
25g grated parmesan
2 tablespoons mayonnaise
¼ teaspoon salt
¼ teaspoon ground black pepper

1. Place 6 whole eggs in the air fryer basket, and cook them in the air fryer at 105°C for 20 minutes. 2. After cooking, place eggs in a bowl of ice water to cool 5 minutes. 3. Peel the eggs, and cut them in half lengthwise; remove the yolks and place the yolks in a medium bowl. 4. Whisk the remaining raw egg in another bowl. Place parmesan in a separate bowl. 5. Dip each egg white into whisked egg, and gently coat with parmesan, then place them in the air fryer basket and spritz with cooking spray. 6. Cook the egg whites at 200°C for 5 minutes until golden, turning them halfway through. 7. Mash egg yolks with the mayonnaise in a clean bowl until smooth, then mix in the salt and pepper. 8. Spoon 2 tablespoons of yolk mixture into each fried egg white, then enjoy.
Per Serving: Calories 126; Fat 8.62g; Sodium 304mg; Carbs 0.65g; Fibre 0.1g; Sugar 0.26g; Protein 10.54g

Bacon-Wrapped Cabbage Bites with Sauce

Prep Time: 10 minutes | **Cook Time:** 12 minutes | **Serves:** 6

3 tablespoons sriracha hot chili sauce, divided
1 medium head cabbage, cored and cut into 12 bite-sized pieces
2 tablespoons coconut oil, melted
½ teaspoon salt
12 slices bacon
110g mayonnaise
¼ teaspoon garlic powder

1. Evenly brush the cabbage pieces with 2 tablespoons of sriracha. Drizzle them with coconut oil, and then sprinkle with salt. 2. Wrap one cabbage piece with one bacon slice, and secure with a toothpick. 3. Place the wrapped cabbage pieces in the air fryer basket, and cook them in the air fryer at 190°C for 12 minutes until the bacon slices are crispy, turning them halfway through. 4. Mix the mayonnaise, garlic powder, and remaining sriracha in a small dish, and then enjoy the cabbage pieces with the mayonnaise sauce.
Per Serving: Calories 198; Fat 12.66g; Sodium 799mg; Carbs 8.7g; Fibre 2.3g; Sugar 4.5g; Protein 14.17g

Bacon Cauliflower Skewers

Prep Time: 10 minutes | **Cook Time:** 12 minutes | **Serves:** 4

4 slices bacon, cut into thirds
¼ medium yellow onion, peeled and cut into 2 cm pieces
100g (about 8) cauliflower florets
1½ tablespoons olive oil
¼ teaspoon salt
¼ teaspoon garlic powder

1. Place 1 bacon piece and 2 onion pieces on a 15 cm skewer. Add a second piece bacon, and 2 cauliflower florets, followed by another piece of bacon onto skewer. 2. Do the same with the remaining ingredients and three additional skewers to make four total skewers. 3. Drizzle the skewers with olive oil, and sprinkle them with salt and garlic powder. 4. Place the skewers in the air fryer basket, and cook them in the air fryer at 190°C for 12 minutes until the vegetables are tender and the bacon slices are crispy, turning them halfway through. 5. Serve hot.
Per Serving: Calories 87; Fat 5.95g; Sodium 366mg; Carbs 2.56g; Fibre 0.7g; Sugar 1.09g; Protein 6.42g

Parmesan Chips

Prep time: 5 minutes| **Cook time:** 20 to 25 minutes| **Serves:** 4

3 medium russet potatoes, rinsed, dried, and cut into thin wedges or classic chip shapes
2 tablespoons extra-virgin olive oil
1 tablespoon granulated garlic
30g grated Parmesan cheese
½ teaspoon salt
¼ teaspoon freshly ground black pepper
Cooking oil spray
2 tablespoons finely chopped fresh parsley (optional)

1. Combine the potato wedges or chips and the olive oil in a suitable bowl. Toss to coat. 2. Sprinkle the potatoes with the granulated garlic, Parmesan cheese, salt, and pepper, and toss them again. 3. Insert the crisper plate into the basket and the basket into the unit. 4. To preheat, set your air fryer on AIR FRY mode and set the temperature to 400°F/ 200°C and time to 3 minutes. 5. Once the unit is preheated, spray the crisper plate with cooking oil. Place the potatoes into the basket. 6. Let it cook on AIR FRY mode at 400°F/ 200°C and for 20 to 25 minutes. 7. Cook it in your air fryer for about 10 minutes, and then remove the basket and shake it, so the chips at the bottom come up to the top. Reinsert the basket to resume cooking. 8. When the cooking is complete, top the chips with the parsley (if using) and serve hot.
Per Serving: Calories 225; Fat 9.2g; Sodium 449mg; Carbs 31g; Fibre 2.2g; Sugar 1g; Protein 6g

Sausage-Stuffed Cremini Mushrooms

Prep Time: 10 minutes | **Cook Time:** 20 minutes | **Serves:** 6

225g pork sausage meat
¼ teaspoon salt
¼ teaspoon garlic powder
2 medium spring onions, trimmed and chopped
10g grated parmesan
455g cremini mushrooms, stems removed

1. Mix the sausage with salt, garlic powder, spring onions, and parmesan in a large bowl. Scoop 1 tablespoon of mixture into centre of each mushroom cap. 2. Place the stuffed mushroom caps in the air fryer basket, and cook them in the air fryer basket at 190°C for 20 minutes until the pork have an internal temperature of at least 60°C. 3. Serve warm.
Per Serving: Calories 132; Fat 10.04g; Sodium 383mg; Carbs 3.28g; Fibre 0.9g; Sugar 0.9g; Protein 8.62g

Ranch Cauliflower Bites

Prep Time: 5 minutes | **Cook Time:** 15 minutes | **Serves:** 6

1 medium head cauliflower, leaves and core removed, cut into bite-sized pieces
4 tablespoons salted butter, melted
30g dry ranch seasoning
80ml buffalo sauce

1. Place cauliflower pieces in a large bowl, coat them with butter and ranch seasoning. 2. Place the cauliflower in the air fryer basket, and cook them in the air fryer at 175°C for 12 minutes, tossing them three times during cooking. 3. Transfer them to a clean large bowl, and toss them with the buffalo sauce, then return them back to the air fryer and cook for 3 minutes more until the edges are darkened and they are tender. 4. Serve warm.
Per Serving: Calories 102; Fat 5.58g; Sodium 283mg; Carbs 12.04g; Fibre 1.3g; Sugar 6.36g; Protein 1.74g

Ranch Chicken Bites

Prep Time: 10 minutes | **Cook Time:** 15 minutes | **Serves:** 6

2 (170g) boneless, skinless chicken breasts, cut into 2-cm cubes
1 tablespoon coconut oil
½ teaspoon salt
¼ teaspoon ground black pepper
80ml ranch dressing
50g shredded Colby cheese
4 slices cooked bacon, crumbled

1. Drizzle the chicken cubes with coconut oil, and sprinkle with salt and pepper, then place them in a suitable baking dish. 2. Place the dish in the air fryer basket, and cook the chicken cubes at 185°C for 10 minutes, stirring them halfway through. 3. When the time is up, drizzle them with the ranch dressing, and top them with Colby and bacon. 4. Cook them again in the air fryer at 200°C for 5 minutes until they are browed and have an internal temperature of at least 75°C. 5. Serve warm.
Per Serving: Calories 180; Fat 14.47g; Sodium 537mg; Carbs 1.47g; Fibre 0g; Sugar 0.94g; Protein 11.55g

Fish and Seafood Recipes

Fried Sardines with Dip

Prep Time: 5 minutes | **Cook Time:** 6 minutes | **Serves:** 2

50g crushed pork crackling
2 (95g) cans skinless, boneless sardines packed in oil, drained
120ml warmed romesco sauce

1. Preheat the air fryer to 175°C. Lightly grease the air fryer basket with olive oil. 2. Place pork crackling in a shallow dish, and coat the sardines with pork crackling. 3. Place coated sardines in air fryer basket, and cook them for 6 minutes, flipping them halfway through. 4. Serve warm with romesco sauce.
Per Serving: Calories 372; Fat 31.76g; Sodium 769mg; Carbs 4.37g; Fibre 1.2g; Sugar 2.56g; Protein 16.82g

Lemon Sea Bass

Prep Time: 5 minutes | **Cook Time:** 7 minutes | **Serves:** 2

1 tablespoon butter, melted
2 cloves garlic, peeled and minced
1 tablespoon fresh lemon juice
¼ teaspoon salt
2 (150g, 2cm thick) sea bass fillets
2 teaspoons chopped fresh parsley

1. Preheat the air fryer at 190°C for 3 minutes. 2. Mix butter, garlic, lemon juice, and salt in a small bowl, and then rub the tops of fillets with this butter mixture. 3. Place the sea bass in air fryer basket, and cook them for 7 minutes. 4. Let the sea bass rest for 5 minutes after transferring to the serving plates, then garnish them with the chopped parsley, and enjoy.
Per Serving: Calories 124; Fat 5.6g; Sodium 352mg; Carbs 1.6g; Fibre 0.1g; Sugar 0.23g; Protein 16.16g

Pesto Prawns with Pilaf

Prep Time: 5 minutes | **Cook Time:** 5 minutes | **Serves:** 4

450g medium prawns, peeled and deveined
4 tablespoons pesto sauce
1 lemon, sliced
300g cooked wild rice pilaf

1. Preheat the air fryer to 180°C. 2. Toss the prawns with the pesto sauce in a bowl until well coated. 3. Place the prawns in a single layer in the air fryer basket, and top them with lemon slices. 4. Roast the prawns for 5 minutes. 5. After roasting, discard the lemons. Serve a quarter of the prawns over 75g wild rice with some favorite steamed vegetables.
Per Serving: Calories 342; Fat 14.08g; Sodium 1293mg; Carbs 33.03g; Fibre 0.9g; Sugar 0.74g; Protein 20.49g

Roasted Sea Bass with Vegetables

Prep Time: 10 minutes | **Cook Time:** 15 minutes | **Serves:** 4

1 carrot, diced small
1 parsnip, diced small
1 turnip diced small
60ml olive oil
2 teaspoons salt, divided
4 sea bass fillets
½ teaspoon onion powder
2 garlic cloves, minced
1 lemon, sliced, plus additional wedges for serving

1. Preheat the air fryer to 195°C. 2. Toss the carrot, parsnip, and turnip with olive oil and 1 teaspoon of salt. 3. Lightly season each sea bass with onion powder and the remaining 1 teaspoon of salt, then place them in the air fryer basket in a single layer, then spread the garlic over them, and cover them with lemon slices. 4. Pour the prepared vegetables into the basket around and on top of the fish. 5. Roast the food for 15 minutes. 6. Serve the fillets with additional lemon wedges if desired.
Per Serving: Calories 298; Fat 16.33g; Sodium 1269mg; Carbs 12.88g; Fibre 3.2g; Sugar 4.67g; Protein 24.98g

Fish-Pork Sticks

Prep time: 15 minutes| **Cook time:** 12 minutes| **Serves:** 4

1 large egg
½ teaspoon Old Bay Seasoning
42g plain pork crackling, finely crushed
4 (113g) cod fillets, cut into 1" × 2" sticks

1. In a medium bowl, whisk the egg. In a separate medium bowl, combine the Old Bay Seasoning and pork cracklings. 2. Dip each fish stick into the egg, then gently press it into the pork crackling mixture to coat all sides. Place the fish sticks into an ungreased air fryer basket. Adjust the temperature setting to 400°F/ 200°C and set the timer for 12 minutes, turning the fish sticks halfway through cooking. The fish sticks will be golden brown and have an internal temperature of at least 145°F/ 60°C when done. Serve warm.
Per Serving: Calories 189; Fat 8g; Sodium 436mg; Carbs 0.5g; Fibre 0g; Sugar 0.2g; Protein 26.6g

Homemade Ahi Tuna Steaks

Prep time: 5 minutes| **Cook time:** 14 minutes| **Serves:** 2

2 (170g) ahi tuna steaks
2 tablespoons olive oil
3 tablespoons everything bagel seasoning

1. Drizzle both sides of each steak with olive oil. Place seasoning on a medium plate and press each side of tuna steaks into seasoning to form a thick layer. 2. Place steaks into an ungreased air fryer basket. Adjust the temperature setting to 400°F/ 200°C and set the timer for 14 minutes, turning steaks halfway through cooking. Steaks will be done when the internal temperature is at least 145°F/ 60°C for well-done. Serve warm.
Per Serving: Calories 189; Fat 8g; Sodium 436mg; Carbs 0.5g; Fibre 0g; Sugar 0.2g; Protein 26.6g

Italian Marinara Cod Bake

Prep time: 5 minutes| **Cook time:** 12 minutes| **Serves:** 4

4 (170g) cod fillets
2 tablespoons salted butter, melted
1 teaspoon Italian seasoning
¼ teaspoon salt
½ cup low-carb marinara sauce

1. Place the cod into an ungreased 6" round non-stick baking dish. Pour the butter over cod and sprinkle with Italian seasoning and salt. Top with marinara. 2. Place the dish into an air fryer basket. Adjust the temperature setting to 350°F/ 175°C and set the timer for 12 minutes. The fillets will be lightly browned, easily flake, and have an internal temperature of at least 145°F/ 60°C when done. Serve warm.
Per Serving: Calories 170; Fat 5g; Sodium 754mg; Carbs 3g; Fibre 0g; Sugar 1.8g; Protein 26.5g

Lemony Cod with Olives

Prep time: 5 minutes| **Cook time:** 12 minutes| **Serves:** 4

4 (170g) cod fillets
3 tablespoons fresh lemon juice
1 tablespoon olive oil
¼ teaspoon salt
6 cherry tomatoes, halved
30g pitted and sliced Kalamata olives

1. Place the cod into an ungreased 6" round non-stick baking dish. Pour the lemon juice into a dish and drizzle cod with olive oil. Sprinkle with salt. Place cherry tomatoes and olives around the baking dish in between the fillets. 2. Place the dish into an air fryer basket. Adjust the temperature setting to 350°F/ 175°C and set the timer for 12 minutes, carefully turning cod halfway through cooking. The fillets will be lightly browned, easily flake, and have an internal temperature of at least 145°F/ 60°C when done. Serve warm.
Per Serving: Calories 164; Fat 5g; Sodium 724mg; Carbs 2.3g; Fibre 0.6g; Sugar 1g; Protein 26.3g

Honey-Glazed Salmon Fillets

Prep Time: 5 minutes | **Cook Time:** 12 minutes | **Serves:** 4

85g raw honey
4 garlic cloves, minced
1 tablespoon olive oil
½ teaspoon salt
Olive oil cooking spray
4 (3cm-thick) salmon fillets

1. Preheat the air fryer to 195°C. 2. Mix the honey, garlic, olive oil, and salt in a small bowl. 3. Spray the bottom of the air fryer basket with olive oil cooking spray, and place the salmon in the air fryer basket in a single layer. 4. Brush the fillets with the honey-garlic mixture, and roast for 10 to 12 minutes until they have an internal temperature of 60°C. 5. Serve warm.
Per Serving: Calories 337; Fat 10.91g; Sodium 391mg; Carbs 18.48g; Fibre 0.1g; Sugar 17.44g; Protein 40.13g

Simple and Quick Prawn

Prep time: 2 minutes| **Cook time:** 5 minutes| **Serves:** 4

450g medium prawn, peeled and deveined
2 tablespoons salted butter, melted
¼ teaspoon salt
¼ teaspoon ground black pepper

1. In a large bowl, toss the prawn into the butter, then sprinkle it with salt and pepper. 2. Place the prawn into an ungreased air fryer basket. Adjust the temperature setting to 400°F/ 200°C and set the timer for 5 minutes, shaking the basket halfway through cooking. The prawn will be opaque and pink when done. Serve warm.
Per Serving: Calories 115; Fat 5g; Sodium 818mg; Carbs 1.1g; Fibre 0g; Sugar 0g; Protein 15.5g

Chilli Garlic Prawn

Prep time: 5 minutes| **Cook time:** 5 minutes| **Serves:** 4

450g medium prawn, peeled and deveined
1 tablespoon salted butter, melted
2 teaspoons chilli powder
¼ teaspoon garlic powder
¼ teaspoon salt
¼ teaspoon ground black pepper
½ small lime, zested and juiced, divided

1. In a medium bowl, toss the prawn with butter, then sprinkle with chilli powder, garlic powder, salt, pepper, and lime zest. 2. Place prawn into an ungreased air fryer basket. Adjust the temperature setting to 400°F/ 200°C and set the timer for 5 minutes. The prawn will be firm and form a 'C' shape when done. 3. Transfer the prawn to a large serving dish and drizzle with lime juice. Serve warm.
Per Serving: Calories 104; Fat 3.3g; Sodium 842mg; Carbs 2.4g; Fibre 0.5g; Sugar 0.2g; Protein 15.7g

Crispy Coconut Prawn

Prep time: 5 minutes| **Cook time:** 8 minutes| **Serves:** 2

250g jumbo prawn, peeled and deveined
2 tablespoons salted butter, melted
½ teaspoon Old Bay Seasoning
20g unsweetened shredded coconut
30g coconut flour

1. In a large bowl, toss the prawns into the butter and Old Bay Seasoning. 2. In a medium bowl, combine the shredded coconut with the coconut flour. Coat each prawn in the coconut mixture. 3. Place the prawns into an ungreased air fryer basket. Adjust the temperature setting to 400°F/ 200°C and set the timer for 8 minutes, gently turning the prawns halfway through cooking. The prawns will be pink and C-shaped when done. Serve warm.
Per Serving: Calories 268; Fat 13g; Sodium 1051mg; Carbs 12.4g; Fibre 2.5g; Sugar g; Protein g

Crab-Avocado Boats

Prep time: 5 minutes| **Cook time:** 7 minutes| **Serves:** 4

2 medium avocados, halved and pitted
230g cooked crab meat
¼ teaspoon Old Bay Seasoning
2 tablespoons peeled and diced yellow onion
2 tablespoons mayonnaise

1. Scoop out the avocado flesh from each avocado half, leaving ½" around the edges to form a shell. Chop the scooped-out avocado. 2. In a medium bowl, combine the crab meat, Old Bay Seasoning, onion, mayonnaise, and chopped avocado. Place ¼ mixture into each avocado shell. 3. Place the avocado boats into an ungreased air fryer basket. Adjust the temperature setting to 350°F/ 175°C and set the timer for 7 minutes. The avocado will be browned on top, and the mixture will be bubbling when done. Serve warm.
Per Serving: Calories 253; Fat 17.2g; Sodium 66mg; Carbs 27g; Fibre 8g; Sugar 17.2g; Protein 2.7g

Lemon-Butter Lobster Tails

Prep time: 5 minutes| **Cook time:** 9 minutes| **Serves:** 4

4 (170g) lobster tails
2 tablespoons salted butter, melted
1 tablespoon peeled and finely minced garlic
¼ teaspoon salt
¼ teaspoon ground black pepper
2 tablespoons lemon juice

1. Carefully cut open the lobster tails with scissors and pull back the shell a little to expose the meat. Pour butter over each tail, then sprinkle with garlic, salt, and pepper. 2. Place the tails into an ungreased air fryer basket. Adjust the temperature setting to 400°F/ 200°C and set the timer for 9 minutes. The lobster will be firm and opaque when done. 3. Transfer the tails to four medium plates and pour lemon juice over the lobster meat. Serve warm.
Per Serving: Calories 268; Fat 6g; Sodium 1436mg; Carbs 1.3g; Fibre 0g; Sugar 0.2g; Protein 49.4g

Old Bay Tuna Cakes

Prep time: 10 minutes| **Cook time:** 10 minutes| **Serves:** 4

4 (85g) pouches tuna, drained
1 large egg, whisked
15g peeled and chopped white onion
½ teaspoon Old Bay seasoning

1. In a large bowl, mix the tuna, 1 egg, white onion, and Old Bay seasoning together and form into four patties. 2. Place the patties into an ungreased air fryer basket. Adjust the temperature setting to 400°F/ 200°C and set the timer for 10 minutes. The patties will be browned and crispy when done. Let cool for 5 minutes before serving.
Per Serving: Calories 113; Fat 1.6g; Sodium 56mg; Carbs 0.6g; Fibre 0g; Sugar 0.3g; Protein 22.4g

Baked Salmon Burgers with Broccoli Slaw

Prep Time: 15 minutes | **Cook Time:** 10 minutes | **Serves:** 4

For the salmon burgers
455g salmon fillets, bones and skin removed
1 egg
3g fresh dill, chopped
90g whole wheat bread crumbs
1 teaspoon salt
½ teaspoon cayenne pepper
2 garlic cloves, minced
4 whole wheat buns

For the broccoli slaw
270g chopped or shredded broccoli
20g shredded carrots
30g sunflower seeds
2 garlic cloves, minced
½ teaspoon salt
2 tablespoons apple cider vinegar
245g nonfat plain Greek yogurt

1. Preheat the air fryer to 180°C. 2. Pulse the salmon fillets in a food processor until they are finely chopped. 3. Combine the chopped salmon, egg, dill, bread crumbs, salt, cayenne, and garlic in a large bowl, then make the mixture into 4 patties. 4. Place them into the air fryer basket, making sure that they don't touch each other. 5. Bake them for 10 minutes, flipping them halfway through. 6. In a large bowl, combine all of the ingredients for the broccoli slaw. 7.Serve the salmon burgers on toasted whole wheat buns, and top with a generous portion of broccoli slaw.
Per Serving: Calories 457; Fat 16.19g; Sodium 1732mg; Carbs 41.08g; Fibre 5.4g; Sugar 3.94g; Protein 37.15g

Baked Grouper with Tomatoes

Prep Time: 5 minutes | **Cook Time:** 12 minutes | **Serves:** 4

4 grouper fillets
½ teaspoon salt
3 garlic cloves, minced
1 tomato, sliced
35g sliced Kalamata olives
3g fresh dill, roughly chopped
Juice of 1 lemon
60ml olive oil

1. Preheat the air fryer to 195°C. 2. Season the grouper fillets with salt on all sides, then place them in the air fryer basket, and top with the minced garlic, tomato slices, olives, and fresh dill. 3. Drizzle the grouper with the lemon juice and olive oil, and bake them for 10 to 12 minutes until they have an internal temperature of 60°C. 4. Serve warm.
Per Serving: Calories 374; Fat 17.09g; Sodium 491mg; Carbs 2.28g; Fibre 0.4g; Sugar 0.42g; Protein 50.5g

Steamed Cod with Swiss Chard

Prep Time: 5 minutes | **Cook Time:** 12 minutes | **Serves:** 4

1 teaspoon salt
½ teaspoon dried oregano
½ teaspoon dried thyme
½ teaspoon garlic powder
4 cod fillets
½ white onion, thinly sliced
70g Swiss chard, washed, stemmed, and torn into pieces
60ml olive oil
1 lemon, quartered

1. Preheat the air fryer to 195°C. 2. Mix the salt, oregano, thyme, and garlic powder in a small bowl. 3. Tear off four pieces of aluminum foil, with each sheet being large enough to envelop one cod fillet and a quarter of the vegetables. 4. Place a cod fillet in the middle of each sheet of foil, then sprinkle on all sides with the spice mixture. 5. In each foil packet, place a quarter of the onion slices and 20 g Swiss chard, then drizzle 1 tablespoon olive oil and squeeze ¼ lemon over the contents of each foil packet. 6. Fold and seal the sides of the foil packets, and then place them into the air fryer basket. 7. Steam them for 12 minutes. 8. After cooking, carefully open each packet to avoid a steam burn. Enjoy.
Per Serving: Calories 220; Fat 14.08g; Sodium 975mg; Carbs 5.03g; Fibre 0.8g; Sugar 2.59g; Protein 18.49g

Fish Pitas with Yogurt

Prep Time: 10 minutes | **Cook Time:** 15 minutes | **Serves:** 4

455g pollock fillets, cut into 2cm pieces
60ml olive oil
1 teaspoon salt
½ teaspoon dried oregano
½ teaspoon dried thyme
½ teaspoon garlic powder
¼ teaspoon cayenne
4 whole wheat pitas
30g shredded lettuce
2 Roma tomatoes, diced
Nonfat plain Greek yogurt
Lemon, quartered

1. Preheat the air fryer to 195°C. 2. Combine the pollock with olive oil, salt, oregano, thyme, garlic powder, and cayenne in a medium bowl. 3. Put the pollock into the air fryer basket, and roast them for 15 minutes. 4.Serve inside pitas with lettuce, tomato, and Greek yogurt with a lemon wedge on the side.
Per Serving: Calories 279; Fat 14.93g; Sodium 1090mg; Carbs 19.65g; Fibre 3.1g; Sugar 2.54g; Protein 18.16g

Prawn Pasta with Mushrooms

Prep Time: 10 minutes | **Cook Time:** 10 minutes | **Serves:** 6

455g small prawns, peeled and deveined
60ml plus 1 tablespoon olive oil, divided
¼ teaspoon garlic powder
¼ teaspoon cayenne
455g whole grain pasta
5 garlic cloves, minced
200g baby bella mushrooms, sliced
50g Parmesan, plus more for serving (optional)
1 teaspoon salt
½ teaspoon black pepper
10g fresh basil

1. Preheat the air fryer to 195°C. 2. Toss the prawn with 1 tablespoon of olive oil, garlic powder, and cayenne in a small bowl. 3. Place the prawn in the air fryer basket, and roast them for 5 minutes. 4. Transfer the prawn to a bowl after roasting, and set aside. 5. Cook the pasta according to package directions. Once done cooking, reserve 120 ml pasta water, then drain. 6. Heat 60 ml of olive oil in a large skillet over medium heat; add the garlic and mushrooms, and cook them for 5 minutes. 7. Add the pasta, reserved pasta water, Parmesan, salt, pepper, and basil to the skillet with the vegetable-and-oil mixture, and stir to coat the pasta. 8. Toss in the prawn and remove the skillet from heat, then let the mixture sit for 5 minutes. 9. You can enjoy with additional Parmesan, if desired.
Per Serving: Calories 432; Fat 7.35g; Sodium 1311mg; Carbs 74.61g; Fibre 10.1g; Sugar 1.6g; Protein 24.3g

Balsamic Prawn

Prep Time: 5 minutes | **Cook Time:** 8 minutes | **Serves:** 4

120ml olive oil
4 garlic cloves, minced
1 tablespoon balsamic vinegar
¼ teaspoon cayenne pepper
¼ teaspoon salt
1 Roma tomato, diced
35g Kalamata olives
455g medium prawns, cleaned and deveined

1. Preheat the air fryer to 195°C. 2. Combine the olive oil, garlic, balsamic, cayenne, and salt in a small bowl. 3. Divide the tomatoes and olives among four small ramekins, then divide prawn among the ramekins, and pour a quarter of the oil mixture over the prawn. 4. Roast them for 6 to 8 minutes until the prawns are cooked through. 5. Serve warm.
Per Serving: Calories 262; Fat 28g; Sodium 211mg; Carbs 3.47g; Fibre 0.7g; Sugar 1.45g; Protein 0.57g

Cajun Cod and Prawn Mango Salsa

Prep Time: 10 minutes | **Cook Time:** 10 minutes | **Serves:** 2

For Prawn Mango Salsa
40g chopped cooked prawns
40g peeled and diced mango
1 medium Roma tomato, cored, seeded, and diced
2 tablespoons peeled and diced red onion
1 tablespoon chopped fresh parsley
2 teaspoons fresh lime juice
¼ teaspoon salt
¼ teaspoon freshly ground black pepper
For Cod
2 (170g) cod fillets
2 teaspoons Cajun seasoning

1. To make the prawn mango salsa, combine all ingredients in a medium bowl, then cover the bowl and refrigerate the salsa until ready to use. 2. Preheat the air fryer to 175°C. Lightly grease the air fryer basket with olive oil. 3. Season the cod fillets with Cajun seasoning, and then place them in the air fryer basket. 4. Cook the cod fillets for 10 minutes until opaque and flake easily with a fork. 5. Apportion them between two medium plates, top them with the refrigerated prawn mango salsa, and enjoy.
Per Serving: Calories 114; Fat 0.81g; Sodium 898mg; Carbs 8.84g; Fibre 1.8g; Sugar 5.27g; Protein 17.32g

Baked Salmon with Tomatoes

Prep Time: 5 minutes | **Cook Time:** 8 minutes | **Serves:** 4

2 tablespoons olive oil
4 (4cm-thick) salmon fillets
½ teaspoon salt
¼ teaspoon cayenne
1 teaspoon chopped fresh dill
2 Roma tomatoes, diced
35g sliced Kalamata olives
4 lemon slices

1. Preheat the air fryer to 195°C. 2. Brush the salmon fillets with olive oil on both sides, then season them lightly with salt, cayenne, and dill. 3. Place the fillets in a single layer in the air fryer basket, then top them with the tomatoes, olives, and top each fillet with a lemon slice. 4. Bake them for 8 minutes until each fillet has reached an internal temperature of 60°C. 5. Serve warm.
Per Serving: Calories 212; Fat 11.72g; Sodium 406mg; Carbs 6.59g; Fibre 1.3g; Sugar 2.84g; Protein 20.86g

Pepper Trout with Lemon Wedges

Prep Time: 5 minutes | **Cook Time:** 15 minutes | **Serves:** 4

4 trout fillets
2 tablespoons olive oil
½ teaspoon salt
1 teaspoon black pepper
2 garlic cloves, sliced
1 lemon, sliced, plus additional wedges for serving

1. Preheat the air fryer to 195°C. 2. Brush each fillet with olive oil on both sides, and season them with salt and pepper. 3. Place them in the air fryer basket in a single layer, and top them the sliced garlic and lemon slices. 4. Roast the fillets for 12 to 15 minutes until they have an internal temperature of 60°C. 5. Serve the fillets with fresh lemon wedges.
Per Serving: Calories 256; Fat 12.31g; Sodium 341mg; Carbs 1.79g; Fibre 0.3g; Sugar 0.32g; Protein 32.78g

Prawn Pita

Prep Time: 5 minutes | **Cook Time:** 8 minutes | **Serves:** 4

450g medium prawns, peeled and deveined
2 tablespoons olive oil
1 teaspoon dried oregano
½ teaspoon dried thyme
½ teaspoon garlic powder
¼ teaspoon onion powder
½ teaspoon salt
¼ teaspoon black pepper
4 whole wheat pitas
120g feta cheese, crumbled
35g shredded lettuce
1 tomato, diced
45g black olives, sliced
1 lemon

1. Preheat the air fryer to 195°C. 2. Combine the prawns, olive oil, oregano, thyme, garlic powder, onion powder, salt, and black pepper in a bowl. 3. Transfer the prawns to the air fryer basket in a single layer, and roast them for 6 to 8 minutes. 4. After roasting, divide the prawns into warmed pitas with feta, lettuce, tomato, olives, and a squeeze of lemon. Enjoy.
Per Serving: Calories 303; Fat 14.8g; Sodium 1320mg; Carbs 20.64g; Fibre 2.9g; Sugar 2.66g; Protein 22.83g

Roasted Whole Red Snapper

Prep Time: 5 minutes | **Cook Time:** 35 minutes | **Serves:** 4

1 teaspoon salt
½ teaspoon black pepper
½ teaspoon ground cumin
¼ teaspoon cayenne
1 (455g – 700g) whole red snapper, cleaned and patted dry
2 tablespoons olive oil
2 garlic cloves, minced
3g fresh dill
Lemon wedges, for serving

1. Preheat the air fryer to 180°C. 2. Mix the salt, pepper, cumin, and cayenne in a small dish. 3. Coat the outside of the fish with olive oil, and sprinkle with the seasoning blend. Stuff the minced garlic and dill inside the cavity of the fish. 4. Place the snapper in air fryer basket, and roast for 35 minutes; after 20 minutes of cooking time, flip the snapper over, and roast for 15 minutes more, or until the snapper reaches an internal temperature of 60°C. 7. Serve warm.
Per Serving: Calories 122; Fat 7.62g; Sodium 618mg; Carbs 1.79g; Fibre 0.2g; Sugar 0.34g; Protein 11.44g

Spiced Tuna Steaks

Prep Time: 5 minutes | **Cook Time:** 9 minutes | **Serves:** 4

1 teaspoon garlic powder
½ teaspoon salt
¼ teaspoon dried thyme
¼ teaspoon dried oregano
4 tuna steaks
2 tablespoons olive oil
1 lemon, quartered

1. Preheat the air fryer to 195°C. 2. Mix the garlic powder, salt, thyme, and oregano in a small bowl. 3. Coat the tuna steaks with olive oil, and season them with seasoning blend on both sides. 4. Place the tuna steaks in the air fryer basket in a single layer. 5. Cook the tuna steaks for 9 minutes; after 5 minutes of cooking time, flip them, and then resume cooking. 6. Serve warm.
Per Serving: Calories 269; Fat 8.79g; Sodium 365mg; Carbs 1.46g; Fibre 0.1g; Sugar 0.32g; Protein 43.74g

Crusted Cod

Prep Time: 10 minutes | **Cook Time:** 10 minutes | **Serves:** 2

50g crushed pork crackling
⅛ teaspoon salt
1 tablespoon Dijon mustard
1 teaspoon fresh lemon juice
1 tablespoon butter, melted
2 (150g) cod fillets

1. Preheat the air fryer to 175°C. 2. Combine the pork crackling, salt, mustard, lemon juice, and butter in a small bowl. 3. Press the mixture evenly across tops of cod fillets. 4. Place cod fillets in air fryer basket lightly greased with olive oil. 5. Cook them for 10 minutes until opaque and flakes easily with a fork. 6. Serve warm.
Per Serving: Calories 341; Fat 30.04g; Sodium 649mg; Carbs 0.63g; Fibre 0.3g; Sugar 0.14g; Protein 16.25g

Tilapia Roulade

Prep Time: 15 minutes | **Cook Time:** 6 minutes | **Serves:** 4

4 (140g) tilapia fillets
1 large egg
2 tablespoons water
40g crushed cornflakes
1 teaspoon salt
½ teaspoon freshly ground black pepper
4 teaspoons pesto
2 tablespoons butter, melted
4 lime wedges

1. Gently pound tilapia fillets between two parchment pieces until "rollable" about ½ cm thickness. 2. In a small bowl, Beat the egg and water in a small bowl. 3. In a shallow dish, Combine the cornflakes, salt, and pepper in a shallow dish. 4. Preheat the air fryer to 175°C. Lightly grease the air fryer basket with oil. 5. Spread 1 teaspoon pesto on each fish fillet. Tightly and gently roll a fillet from one short end to the other. Secure with a toothpick. 6. Do the same with the remaining fillet. 7. Roll each fillet in egg mixture and dredge in cornflake mixture. 8. Place fish in the air fryer basket, and drizzle tops with melted butter, then cook them 6 minutes. 9. After cooking, transfer them to a serving dish, and let rest 5 minutes. 10. Remove toothpicks, and serve warm with lime wedges.
Per Serving: Calories 220; Fat 8.25g; Sodium 835mg; Carbs 12.19g; Fibre 2.1g; Sugar 3.83g; Protein 26.49g

Poultry Recipes

Jerk Chicken Pepper Kebabs

Prep Time: 10 minutes | **Cook Time:** 14 minutes | **Serves:** 4

200g boneless, skinless chicken thighs, cut into 2 cm cubes
2 tablespoons jerk seasoning
2 tablespoons coconut oil
½ medium red pepper, seeded and cut into 2-cm pieces
¼ medium red onion, peeled and cut into 2-cm pieces
½ teaspoon salt

1. Coat the chicken cubes with jerk seasoning and coconut oil on all sides. 2. Using eight 15 cm skewers, build skewers by alternating chicken, pepper, and onion pieces, about three repetitions per skewer. 3. Sprinkle salt over skewers and place them in air fryer basket. 4. Cook the skewers at 185°C for 14 minutes until the chicken cubes are golden and have an internal temperature of at least 75°C, turning skewers halfway through cooking. 5. Serve warm.
Per Serving: Calories 176; Fat 10.04g; Sodium 857mg; Carbs 15.43g; Fibre 1.7g; Sugar 4.1g; Protein 5.61g

Tangy Chicken Wings

Prep Time: 5 minutes | **Cook Time:** 25 minutes | **Serves:** 4

450g bone-in chicken wings, separated at joints
4 tablespoons yellow mustard
½ teaspoon salt
¼ teaspoon ground black pepper

1. Coat the chicken wings with mustard in a large bowl, then sprinkle them with salt and pepper. 2. Place the chicken wings in air fryer basket. 3. Cook the chicken wings at 200°C for 25 minutes, shaking the basket three times during cooking. 4. Wings will be done when browned and cooked to an internal temperature of at least 75°C. 5. Serve warm.
Per Serving: Calories 153; Fat 4.54g; Sodium 555mg; Carbs 1.02g; Fibre 0.7g; Sugar 0.14g; Protein 25.51g

Easy Chicken Breasts

Prep Time: 5 minutes | **Cook Time:** 10 minutes | **Serves:** 4

2 teaspoons olive oil
2 (220g) boneless, skinless chicken breasts
½ teaspoon salt
¼ teaspoon freshly ground black pepper

1. Preheat the air fryer at 175°C for 3 minutes. 2. Lightly brush the chicken breasts with olive oil on both sides, then season them with salt and pepper. 3. Add chicken breasts to the air fryer basket, and cook them for 9 minutes until they have an internal temperature of at least 75°C, shaking the basket and flipping the chicken breasts halfway through. 4. Let the chicken breasts cool for 5 minutes after cooking, then chop into 2-cm cubes and store covered and refrigerated up to 7 days.
Per Serving: Calories 88; Fat 3.74g; Sodium 898mg; Carbs 0.1g; Fibre 0g; Sugar 0g; Protein 12.77g

Turmeric Chicken Thighs

Prep Time: 5 minutes | **Cook Time:** 25 minutes | **Serves:** 4

4 (100g) boneless, skin-on chicken thighs
2 tablespoons coconut oil, melted
½ teaspoon ground turmeric
½ teaspoon salt
½ teaspoon garlic powder
½ teaspoon ground ginger
¼ teaspoon ground black pepper

1. Place chicken thighs in a large bowl and drizzle with coconut oil. Sprinkle with remaining ingredients and toss to coat both sides of thighs. 2. Place thighs in air fryer basket with skin-side up. 3. Cook the chicken wings at 200°C for 25 minutes. 4. After 10 minutes, turn thighs. When there are 5 minutes left, flip thighs once more. 5. Chicken will be done when skin is golden brown and the internal temperature is at least 75°C. 6. Serve warm.
Per Serving: Calories 125; Fat 11.54g; Sodium 314mg; Carbs 0.89g; Fibre 0.2g; Sugar 0.03g; Protein 4.82g

Pecan-Crusted Chicken Breasts

Prep Time: 5 minutes | **Cook Time:** 25 minutes | **Serves:** 4

2 (150g) boneless, skinless chicken breasts, halved lengthwise
60g Low-Carb Honey Mustard
30g finely chopped pecans

1. Preheat the air fryer at 175°C for 3 minutes. Lightly grease the air fryer basket with cooking oil. 2. Coat chicken breasts with Low-Carb Honey Mustard. 3. Place pecans in a shallow dish, and then dredge the chicken breasts in pecans. 4. Add chicken breasts to air fryer basket, and cook them for 10 minutes. 5. Gently flip the chicken breasts and cook an additional 15 minutes until they have an internal temperature of at least 75°C. 6. Let the food cool for 5 minutes before serving.
Per Serving: Calories 125; Fat 8.92g; Sodium 199mg; Carbs 1.77g; Fibre 1.2g; Sugar 0.39g; Protein 10.02g

Jumbo Chicken Meatballs

450g chicken thigh mince
1 large egg, whisked
120ml hot sauce, divided
120g crumbled blue cheese
2 tablespoons dry ranch seasoning
¼ teaspoon salt
¼ teaspoon ground black pepper

1. Mix the chicken, egg, 60ml hot sauce, blue cheese, ranch seasoning, salt, and pepper in a large bowl. 2. Divide the mixture into eight equal sections and form each section into a ball. 3. Place the meatballs in air fryer basket, and cook them at 185°C for 15 minutes until they are golden and have an internal temperature of at least 75°C. 4. Transfer meatballs to a large serving dish, and toss with remaining hot sauce. Serve warm.
Per Serving: Calories 345; Fat 24.99g; Sodium 1517mg; Carbs 3.86g; Fibre 0.7g; Sugar 0.96g; Protein 24.27g

Marinated Chicken Wings

Prep time: 5 minutes plus 1 hour for marinating| **Cook time:** 20 minutes| **Serves:** 4

60ml Jamaican jerk marinade
1 teaspoon onion powder
1 teaspoon garlic powder
1 teaspoon salt
900g chicken wings, flats and drums separated

1. In a large bowl, combine the jerk seasoning, onion powder, garlic powder, and salt. Add the chicken wings and toss to coat well. Cover the bowl and then let them marinate in a refrigerator for at least 1 hour. 2. Preheat the air fryer to 400°F/ 200°C. 3. Place the wings in your air fryer basket in a single layer, working in batches as necessary. Cook the wings for 20 minutes, turning halfway through cooking time, until internal temperature reaches at least 165°F/ 75°C. Cool for 5 minutes before serving.
Per Serving: Calories 342; Fat 13g; Sodium 1052mg; Carbs 3g; Fibre 0g; Sugar 1.6g; Protein 50.5g

Gherkin Chicken Wings

Prep time: 5 minutes plus 2 hours for marinating| **Cook time:** 20 minutes| **Serves:** 4

240ml Gherkin juice
900g chicken wings, flats and drums separated
½ teaspoon salt
½ teaspoon ground black pepper
2 teaspoons dry ranch seasoning

1. Combine the Gherkin juice and wings in a resealable plastic bag. Seal the bag and then let them marinate in a refrigerator for 2 hours. 2. Preheat your air fryer to 400°F/ 200°C. 3. In a separate bowl, mix salt, pepper, and ranch seasoning. Remove wings from marinade and toss in dry seasoning. 4. Place the wings in your air fryer basket in a single layer, working in batches as necessary. Cook for 20 minutes, flipping several times while cooking, until wings reach an internal temperature of at least 165°F/ 75°C. Cool for 5 minutes before serving.
Per Serving: Calories 591; Fat 16g; Sodium 1733mg; Carbs 3.8g; Fibre 1g; Sugar 1g; Protein 100g

Ranch Chicken Meatballs

Prep time: 10 minutes| **Cook time:** 12 minutes| **Serves:** 5

450g ground chicken breast
1 (30g) packet dry ranch seasoning
45g plain bread crumbs
40g mayonnaise
5 tablespoons buffalo sauce, divided

1. Preheat your air fryer to 370°F/ 185°C. 2. In a large bowl, mix the chicken, ranch seasoning, bread crumbs, and mayonnaise together. Pour in 2 tablespoons buffalo sauce and stir to combine. 3. Roll the meat mixture into balls, about 2 tablespoons for each, to make twenty meatballs. 4. Place the meatballs in the air fryer basket and cook for 12 minutes, shaking the basket twice during cooking, until brown and internal temperature reaches at least 165°F/ 75°C. 5. Toss the meatballs in the remaining buffalo sauce and serve.
Per Serving: Calories 230; Fat 11.8g; Sodium 346mg; Carbs 8.7g; Fibre 1g; Sugar 1g; Protein 21g

Chicken Thighs with Chunky Salsa

Prep Time: 5 minutes | **Cook Time:** 30 minutes | **Serves:** 2

455g (approximately 4) boneless, skinless chicken thighs
250g mild chunky salsa

1. Preheat the air fryer at 175°C for 3 minutes. 2. Place chicken thighs in square cake barrel, and cover them with salsa. 3. Cook the chicken thighs in the air fryer for 30 minutes until they have an internal temperature of at least 75°C. 4. Transfer the chicken wings to a serving plate, and let rest 5 minutes. 5. Serve warm.
Per Serving: Calories 533; Fat 37.67g; Sodium 1264mg; Carbs 8.57g; Fibre 4g; Sugar 8g; Protein 37.47g

Onion Chicken Meatballs

455g chicken mince
1 large egg
20g crushed barbecue-flavoured pork cracklings
1 tablespoon sour cream
2 teaspoons brown mustard
2 tablespoons peeled and grated yellow onion
2 tablespoons no-sugar-added tomato paste
1 teaspoon ground cumin
1 teaspoon chili powder

1. Preheat the air fryer at 175°C for 3 minutes. Lightly grease the air fryer basket with olive oil. 2. Combine all ingredients in a large bowl, the make the mixture into eighteen meatballs, about 2 tablespoons each. 3. Add half of meatballs to air fryer basket, and cook for 6 minutes. 4. Shake basket and cook them for an additional 2 minutes. 5. Transfer the cooked meatballs to a large serving dish, and do the same with the remaining meatballs. 6. Serve warm.
Per Serving: Calories 397; Fat 31.65g; Sodium 210mg; Carbs 3.06g; Fibre 0.8g; Sugar 1.3g; Protein 23.91g

Strawberry–Glazed Chicken Tenders

Prep Time: 10 minutes | **Cook Time:** 10 minutes | **Serves:** 4

70g sugar-free strawberry preserves
3 tablespoons chopped fresh basil, divided
1 teaspoon pulp-free orange juice
¼ teaspoon salt
¼ teaspoon freshly ground black pepper
455g chicken mini fillets

1. Combine the preserves, 2 tablespoons of basil, orange juice, salt, and pepper in a medium bowl; add chicken, then cover the bowl and refrigerate them for 30 minutes up to overnight. 2. Preheat the air fryer at 175°C for 3 minutes. 3. Add chicken tenderloins to the air fryer basket, and cook them for 4 minutes. 4. Flip the chicken tenderloins and cook for an additional 5 minutes until they have an internal temperature of at least 75°C. 5. Transfer chicken to a large serving plate, and let rest for 5 minutes, then garnish with remaining basil and serve warm.
Per Serving: Calories 128; Fat 3.08g; Sodium 237mg; Carbs 0.38; Fibre 0.1g; Sugar 0.15g; Protein 23.2g

Chicken Strawberries Salad

Prep Time: 10 minutes | **Cook Time:** 18 minutes | **Serves:** 4

2 (approximately 220g) boneless, skinless chicken breasts, cut into 2cm cubes
1 teaspoon salt
¼ teaspoon freshly ground black pepper
165g mayonnaise
1 tablespoon fresh lime juice
55g chopped pecans
60g finely chopped celery
75g hulled and diced strawberries

1. Preheat the air fryer at 175°C for 3 minutes. 2. Season the chicken cubes with salt and pepper. 3. Add half of chicken cubes to air fryer basket, and cook them for 9 minutes until they have an internal temperature of at least 75°C, flipping them halfway through. 4. Do the same with another half of chicken cubes. 5. Let the chicken cubes cool for a while after cooking, then chop them and add to a medium bowl; add the remaining ingredients and mix them well. 6. Cover the bowl, and refrigerate them until ready to eat.
Per Serving: Calories 489; Fat 36.71g; Sodium 1031mg; Carbs 5.28g; Fibre 2.3g; Sugar 1.99g; Protein 34.29g

Alfredo Chicken Breasts

Prep Time: 10 minutes | **Cook Time:** 20 minutes | **Serves:** 4

4 (150g) boneless, skinless chicken breasts
4 teaspoons coconut oil
½ teaspoon salt
¼ teaspoon ground black pepper
4 strips cooked bacon, broken into 24 pieces
120ml Alfredo sauce
110g shredded mozzarella cheese
¼ teaspoon crushed red pepper flakes

1. Cut six horizontal slits in the top of each chicken breast. Drizzle with coconut oil and sprinkle with salt and black pepper. 2. Place the chicken breasts in a suitable round nonstick baking dish. 3. Place 1 bacon piece in each slit in chicken breasts. Pour Alfredo sauce over chicken and sprinkle with mozzarella and red pepper flakes. 4. Place the baking dish in air fryer basket, and cook the food at 185°C for 20 minutes until the chicken breasts have an internal temperature is at least 75°C and cheese is browned. 5. Serve warm.
Per Serving: Calories 224; Fat 13.91g; Sodium 857mg; Carbs 2.74g; Fibre 0.7g; Sugar 0.77g; Protein 21.72g

Spiced Chicken Legs

Prep Time: 10 minutes | **Cook Time:** 36 minutes | **Serves:** 4

1 teaspoon baking powder
1 teaspoon dried mustard
1 teaspoon smoked paprika
1 teaspoon garlic powder
1 teaspoon salt
1 teaspoon freshly ground black pepper
675g (approximately 6) chicken legs
3 tablespoons butter, melted

1. Preheat the air fryer at 190°C for 3 minutes. Lightly grease the air fryer basket with cooking oil. 2. Combine baking powder, dried mustard, paprika, garlic powder, salt, and pepper in a large bowl, then add the chicken legs and toss until coated. 3. Add the chicken legs to air fryer basket, and cook 10 minutes. 4. Lightly brush the chicken with melted butter, flip them and brush the other side, then resume cooking them for 8 minutes more until they have an internal temperature of at least 75°C. 5. You can cook the chicken legs in batches. 6. Let the chicken legs stand for 5 minutes after cooking, then serve warm.
Per Serving: Calories 288; Fat 15.97g; Sodium 829mg; Carbs 2g; Fibre 0.5g; Sugar 0.1g; Protein 33.01g

Buttermilk-Fried Marinated Chicken Thighs

Prep time: 15 minutes| **Cook time:** 1 hour| **Serves:** 4

1 cup buttermilk
2 tablespoons seasoned salt, divided
450g bone-in, skin-on chicken thighs
120g all-purpose flour
30g corn flour

1. Combine the buttermilk and 1 tablespoon of seasoned salt in a large bowl. Add the chicken. Cover the bowl and leave it to marinate in a refrigerator for 30 minutes. 2. Preheat the air fryer to 375°F/ 190°C. 3. Mix the flour, corn flour, and remaining seasoned salt in a separate bowl. Dredge the chicken thighs, one at a time, into the flour mixture, covering completely. 4. Spray the chicken generously with cooking spray. Be sure that no dry spots remain. Place the prepared chicken in your air fryer basket and cook for 30 minutes, turning halfway through the cooking time and spraying any dry spots until the chicken is dark golden brown and crispy. The internal temperature shall reach at least 165°F/ 75°C. Serve warm.
Per Serving: Calories 365; Fat 10g; Sodium 4115mg; Carbs 34g; Fibre 1g; Sugar 3g; Protein 33g

Thyme Chicken Tenders

Prep time: 10 minutes| **Cook time:** 12 minutes| **Serves:** 4

450g boneless, skinless chicken tenders
2 teaspoons paprika
1 teaspoon garlic powder
1 teaspoon salt
½ teaspoon cayenne pepper
½ teaspoon dried thyme
½ teaspoon ground black pepper

1. Preheat the air fryer to 400°F/ 200°C. 2. Place chicken tenders into a large bowl. 3. Mix paprika, garlic powder, salt, cayenne, thyme, and black pepper in a small bowl. Mix the spice mixture with the chicken and then toss to coat. Spritz the chicken with cooking spray. 4. Place the prepared chicken in your air fryer basket and cook for 12 minutes, turning halfway through the cooking time until the chicken is brown at the edges and the internal temperature reaches at least 165°F/ 75°C. Serve warm.
Per Serving: Calories 205; Fat 7g; Sodium 886mg; Carbs 25g; Fibre 2.3g; Sugar 6.2g; Protein 10.9g

Marinara Chicken Casserole

Prep time: 10 minutes| **Cook time:** 20 minutes| **Serves:** 4

250g cubed cooked chicken breast
½ teaspoon salt
¼ teaspoon ground black pepper
180ml marinara sauce
2 teaspoons Italian seasoning, divided
110g shredded mozzarella cheese
50g grated Parmesan cheese

1. Preheat the air fryer to 320°F/ 160°C. 2. Toss the chicken with salt, pepper, marinara, and 1 teaspoon of Italian seasoning in a large bowl. 3. Scrape the mixture into a 6" round baking dish. Top with mozzarella, Parmesan, and the remaining 1 teaspoon of Italian seasoning. 4. Then, place the mixture in your air fryer basket and cook for 20 minutes until the sauce is bubbling and the cheese is brown and melted. Serve warm.
Per Serving: Calories 237; Fat 7g; Sodium 895mg; Carbs 7.5g; Fibre 1.6g; Sugar 3g; Protein 35g

Spicy Chilli Chicken Drumsticks

Prep time: 5 minutes| **Cook time:** 25 minutes| **Serves:** 4

1 teaspoon salt
1 teaspoon chilli powder
1 teaspoon garlic powder
½ teaspoon ground black pepper
½ teaspoon onion powder
8 (110g) chicken drumsticks
240ml barbecue sauce, divided

1. Preheat the air fryer to 375°F/ 190°C. 2. In a large bowl, combine salt, chilli powder, garlic powder, pepper, and onion powder. Add the drumsticks and toss to fully coat. 3. Brush the drumsticks with 180ml barbecue sauce to coat. 4. Place the coated drumsticks in your air fryer basket and cook for 25 minutes, turning three times during cooking, until the drumsticks are brown and the internal temperature reaches at least 165°F/ 75°C. 5. Before serving, brush the remaining 60ml barbecue sauce over drumsticks. Serve warm.
Per Serving: Calories 494; Fat 21.4g; Sodium 1576mg; Carbs 31g; Fibre 1g; Sugar 24g; Protein 42g

Curry Chicken Legs

Prep Time: 10 minutes | **Cook Time:** 36 minutes | **Serves:** 4

185g plain Greek yogurt
1 tablespoon no-sugar-added tomato paste
2 teaspoons curry powder
1 teaspoon salt
680g (approximately 6) chicken legs
2 tablespoons chopped fresh mint

1. Whisk yogurt, tomato paste, curry powder, and salt in a medium bowl. 2. Divide mixture in half. Cover half and place in refrigerator. 3. Add chicken legs to other half and toss until coated, cover them and refrigerate for 30 minutes up to overnight. 4. Preheat the air fryer at 190°C for 3 minutes. Lightly grease the air fryer basket with olive oil. 5. Shake excess marinade from chicken legs. Add half of chicken legs to air fryer basket, and cook them for 10 minutes. 6. Brush chicken lightly with extra yogurt mixture, flip them and brush other side, then cook them for an additional 8 minutes until they have an internal temperature of at least 75°C. 7. Transfer chicken to a large serving plate and let rest for 5 minutes. Do the same with the remaining chicken legs. 8. Garnish with mint and serve warm.
Per Serving: Calories 224; Fat 7.43g; Sodium 755mg; Carbs 2.12g; Fibre 0.7g; Sugar 1.21g; Protein 35.12g

Garlic Chicken Wings

Prep Time: 10 minutes | **Cook Time:** 22 minutes | **Serves:** 4

1 tablespoon water
900g chicken wings, split at the joint
2 tablespoons melted butter, divided
2 tablespoons grated Parmesan cheese
4 cloves garlic, peeled and minced
¼ teaspoon salt

1. Pour water into bottom of air fryer to ensure minimum smoke from fat drippings. Preheat air fryer at 120°C for 3 minutes. 2. Toss wings with 1 tablespoon butter in a large bowl, then place them in air fryer basket. 3. Cook the chicken wings for 12 minutes, flipping them halfway through. 4. While chicken wings are cooking, combine the remaining butter, Parmesan cheese, garlic, and salt in a separate large bowl. 5. When the cooking time is up, increase the cooking temperature to 200°C, flip the chicken wings and resume cooking for 5 minutes more. 6. Flip once more and cook 5 more minutes. 7. Transfer the chicken wings to the bowl with sauce and toss, then transfer to a large serving plate, and serve warm.
Per Serving: Calories 336; Fat 12.6g; Sodium 377mg; Carbs 1.34g; Fibre 0.1g; Sugar 0.03g; Protein 50.96g

Breaded Chicken Drumsticks

Prep Time: 10 minutes | **Cook Time:** 40 minutes | **Serves:** 4

455g chicken drumsticks
60g cassava flour
120g heavy cream
115g sour cream
20g crushed pork cracklings
1 tablespoon Cajun seasoning
2 tablespoons melted butter

1. Toss drumsticks with cassava flour in a large bowl. Shake away excess flour and set aside. 2. Whisk the heavy cream and sour cream in a medium bowl. 3. Combine pork cracklings and Cajun seasoning in a shallow dish. 4. Preheat the air fryer at 190°C for 3 minutes. Lightly grease the air fryer basket with olive oil. 5. Dip floured drumsticks in cream mixture, then dredge them in seasoned pork cracklings. 6. Place half of drumsticks in air fryer basket, and cook them for 12 minutes. 7. Gently flip chicken and brush with 1 tablespoon of butter, then cook them for an additional 8 minutes until they have an internal temperature of at least 75°C. 8. Transfer chicken to a large serving plate and let rest for 5 minutes. Do the same with the remaining chicken. 9. Serve warm.
Per Serving: Calories 421; Fat 28.37g; Sodium 349mg; Carbs 13.51g; Fibre 0.7g; Sugar 1.15g; Protein 26.41g

Chicken Wings in Fish Sauce

Prep Time: 10 minutes | **Cook Time:** 22 minutes | **Serves:** 4

2 tablespoons sesame oil
¼ teaspoon fish sauce
2 teaspoons coconut aminos
2 teaspoons sambal oelek
1 teaspoon sweetener
1 teaspoon fresh lime juice
900g chicken wings, split at the joint
1 tablespoon water

1. Combine sesame oil, fish sauce, coconut aminos, sambal oelek, sweetener, and lime juice in a medium bowl. 2. Divide mixture in half. Toss wings in half of sauce, cover, and refrigerate for 30 minutes. 3. Cover and refrigerate other half. 4. Preheat air fryer at 120°C for 3 minutes. Place water in bottom of air fryer to ensure minimum smoke from fat drippings. 5. Place the chicken wings in air fryer basket, and cook 12 minutes, flipping they halfway through. 6. Raise temperature on air fryer to 200°C, flip the wings and cook for 5 minutes. Then, flip wings once more, and cook for an additional 5 minutes. 7. Transfer the chicken wings to the serving bowl, and toss them with the remaining sauce. Enjoy.
Per Serving: Calories 351; Fat 15.08g; Sodium 255mg; Carbs 0.45g; Fibre 0.1g; Sugar 0.21g; Protein 50.24g

Yellow Mustard Wings

Prep Time: 10 minutes | **Cook Time:** 22 minutes | **Serves:** 4

1 tablespoon water
900g chicken wings, split at the joint
1 tablespoon sesame oil
2 tablespoons spicy yellow mustard
1 tablespoon coconut aminos
1 teaspoon sweetener
1 teaspoon apple cider vinegar

1. Preheat air fryer at 120°C for 3 minutes. Pour water in bottom of air fryer to ensure minimum smoke from fat drippings. 2. Toss wings with sesame oil in a large bowl, the place them in the air fryer basket. 3. Cook chicken wings for 12 minutes, flipping them halfway through cooking. 4. While wings are cooking, combine mustard, coconut aminos, sweetener and apple cider vinegar in a separate large bowl. 5. When the cooking time is up, raise the cooking temperature to 200°C. Flip the chicken wings and cook for 5 minutes, then flip them again and cook for an additional 5 minutes. 6. Transfer the wings to bowl, and toss them with the sauce. Enjoy.
Per Serving: Calories 325; Fat 11.93g; Sodium 293mg; Carbs 0.66g; Fibre 0.4g; Sugar 0.17g; Protein 50.47g

Cheese Chicken Patties

Prep Time: 10 minutes | **Cook Time:** 26 minutes | **Serves:** 4

455g chicken mince
2 tablespoons peeled and diced yellow onion
25g shredded Cheddar cheese
15g chopped fresh parsley
1 large egg white, beaten
¼ teaspoon salt
¼ teaspoon freshly ground black pepper

1. Preheat the air fryer at 175°C for 3 minutes. Lightly grease the air fryer basket with olive oil. 2. Combine all ingredients in a large bowl, then form into four patties, making a slight indentation in the middle of each patty. (Patties tend to puff up in the middle during the cooking process, so making an indentation will ensure the patty doesn't become a meatball.) 3. Add two patties to air fryer basket, and cook 6 minutes. 4. Flip patties and cook an additional 7 minutes until they have an internal temperature of at least 75°C. 5. Transfer cooked patties to a large serving plate, and do the same with the remaining patties. 6. Serve warm.
Per Serving: Calories 264; Fat 17.76g; Sodium 319mg; Carbs 1.64g; Fibre 0.3g; Sugar 0.8g; Protein 23.13g

Chicken-Goat Cheese Balls

Prep Time: 10 minutes | **Cook Time:** 24 minutes | **Serves:** 4

455g chicken mince
2 tablespoons peeled and grated yellow onion
5g chopped fresh basil leaves
35g goat cheese crumbles
20g crushed pork cracklings
½ teaspoon garlic powder

1. Preheat the air fryer at 175°C for 3 minutes. Lightly grease the air fryer basket with olive oil. 2. Combine all ingredients in a large bowl, and form the mixture into eighteen meatballs, about 2 tablespoons each. 3. Add half of balls to air fryer basket, and cook them for 12 minutes, shaking the basket halfway through. 4. Transfer cooked balls to a serving plate, and do the same with the remaining balls. 5. Serve warm.
Per Serving: Calories 398; Fat 32.27g; Sodium 229mg; Carbs 1.06g; Fibre 0.1g; Sugar 0.46g; Protein 24.4g

Chicken Bulgogi with Riced Cauliflower

Prep Time: 15 minutes | **Cook Time:** 11 minutes | **Serves:** 4

For Pickled Cucumbers
1 large English cucumber, thinly sliced
60ml apple cider vinegar
2 cloves garlic, peeled and minced
½ teaspoon ground ginger
⅛ teaspoon red pepper flakes
2 teaspoons granular sweetener
⅛ teaspoon salt

For Chicken Bulgogi
2 tablespoons coconut aminos
2 teaspoons sesame oil
2 teaspoons granular sweetener
1 tablespoon apple cider vinegar
1 tablespoon fresh lime juice
2 cloves garlic, peeled and minced
2 teaspoons peeled and minced fresh ginger
3 spring onions, sliced, whites and greens separated, divided
675g (approximately 6) boneless, skinless chicken thighs, cut into 2cm cubes

Additional Ingredients
500g steamed cauliflower rice
2 teaspoons roasted sesame seeds

1. To make the pickled cucumbers, combine all the pickle cucumber ingredients in a medium bowl, then cover the bowl and refrigerate them until ready to serve. 2. To make chicken Bulgogi, whisk together coconut aminos, sesame oil, sweetener, apple cider vinegar, lime juice, garlic, ginger, and whites of spring onions in a large bowl; add the chicken cubes and marinate for 10 minutes in refrigerator. 3. Preheat the air fryer at 175°C for 3 minutes. 4. Place chicken cubes in the air fryer basket, do not discard excess marinade. 5. Cook the chicken cubes in the air fryer for 11 minutes, shaking basket and pouring the remaining marinade over chicken cubes halfway through. 6. When done, the chicken cubes should have an internal temperature of at least 75°C. 7. To assemble: Serve chicken warm over steamed cauliflower in a large serving dish. Garnish with spring onion greens, pickled cucumbers, and sesame seeds.
Per Serving: Calories 475; Fat 31.84g; Sodium 261mg; Carbs 16.09g; Fibre 3.3g; Sugar 9.16g; Protein 31.39g

Beef, Pork, and Lamb Recipes

Flavourful Pork Ribs

Prep Time: 10 minutes | **Cook Time:** 40 minutes | **Serves:** 4

1 teaspoon smoked paprika
1 teaspoon garlic powder
1 teaspoon dark brown sugar
½ teaspoon ground mustard
1 teaspoon salt
½ teaspoon ground black pepper
2 tablespoons water
2 tablespoons olive oil
900g country-style pork ribs

1. Combine smoked paprika, garlic powder, brown sugar, ground mustard, salt, and pepper in a small bowl. 2. Preheat the air fryer at 175°C for 3 minutes. Lightly grease the air fryer basket with cooking oil. Add water to bottom of air fryer. 3. Massage olive oil into pork ribs, and season ribs with spice mixture. 4. Add pork to air fryer basket, and cook them for 40 minutes, flipping every 10 minutes. 5. Transfer cooked pork to a serving platter and serve warm.
Per Serving: Calories 389; Fat 19.72g; Sodium 735mg; Carbs 2.6g; Fibre 0.4g; Sugar 1.5g; Protein 47.47g

Tacos with Pineapple Salsa

Prep Time: 15 minutes | **Cook Time:** 7 minutes | **Serves:** 3

For Pineapple Salsa
165g diced pineapple
120ml fresh lime juice
1 tablespoon lime zest
2 medium Roma tomatoes, seeded and diced
30g finely diced peeled red onion
1 medium avocado, peeled, pitted, and diced
15g chopped fresh cilantro
5g chopped fresh mint
1 teaspoon salt
For Tacos
1 (340g) can SPAM, sliced into ½cm-thick fries
200g coleslaw mix
1 batch Sriracha Mayonnaise
6 (12cm) gluten-free flour tortillas

1. To make pineapple salsa, combine salsa ingredients in a medium bowl, then cover the bowl and refrigerate them until ready to use. 2. Preheat the air fryer at 190°C for 3 minutes. Lightly grease the air fryer basket with cooking oil. 3. Place SPAM fries in air fryer basket, and cook them for 3 minutes. 4. Flip fries, and cook for an additional 4 minutes. Transfer to a large plate after cooking. 5. Build tacos by adding cooked SPAM, coleslaw mix, pineapple salsa, and a squeeze of l to tortillas. Enjoy.
Per Serving: Calories 682; Fat 23.8g; Sodium 1574mg; Carbs 81.11g; Fibre 8.9g; Sugar 20.69g; Protein 38.55g

Bacon and Cheese Ranch Pinwheels

Prep time: 10 minutes| **Cook time:** 12 minutes| **Serves:** 5

110g full-fat cream cheese, softened
1 tablespoon dry ranch seasoning
55g shredded Cheddar cheese
1 (230g) sheet frozen puff pastry dough, thawed
6 slices bacon, cooked and crumbled

1. Preheat your air fryer to 320°F/ 160°C. Cut parchment paper to fit the air fryer basket. 2. In a medium bowl, mix the cream cheese, ranch seasoning, and Cheddar. Unfold puff pastry and gently spread cheese mixture over pastry. 3. Sprinkle the crumbled bacon on top. Roll the dough into a log from a long side, pressing in the edges to seal. 4. Cut the log into ten pieces, then place it on the parchment in the air fryer basket, working in batches as necessary. 5. Cook for 12 minutes, turning each piece after 7 minutes. Let cool for 5 minutes before serving.
Per Serving: Calories 474; Fat 37g; Sodium 538mg; Carbs 24g; Fibre 0g; Sugar 2g; Protein 11.8g

Steak Quesadillas

Prep Time: 15 minutes | **Cook Time:** 30 minutes | **Serves:** 4

1 teaspoon chili powder
½ teaspoon smoked paprika
½ teaspoon ground cumin
¼ teaspoon garlic powder
½ teaspoon salt
¼ teaspoon ground black pepper
1 (340g) ribeye steak, 2cm thick
2 teaspoons olive oil
1 small red pepper, seeded and diced
1 small green pepper, seeded and diced
½ medium red onion, peeled and sliced
165g corn kernels
3 tablespoons butter, melted
8 (15cm) gluten-free flour tortillas
220g grated Monterey jack cheese

1. Combine chili powder, smoked paprika, cumin, garlic powder, salt, and black pepper in a small bowl, then rub ribeye steak with mixture on all sides. 2. Cover the bowl, and refrigerate the ribeye steak for 30 minutes. 3. Preheat the air fryer at 200°C for 3 minutes. Lightly grease the air fryer basket with cooking oil. 4. Cook the steak for 10 minutes until it reaches the doneness of medium rare, flipping it halfway through. 5. Transfer steak to a cutting board and let rest 5 minutes. 6. While steak is resting, sauté olive oil with peppers and onion in a large skillet over medium-high heat for 7 minutes until peppers are tender. Toss in corn. Set aside. 7. Thinly slice steak against the grain. 8. Preheat air fryer to 175°C for 3 minutes. 9. Lightly brush melted butter on one side of a tortilla. Place tortilla butter side down in ungreased air fryer basket. Layer one-quarter steak on tortilla, followed by one-quarter pepper mixture and one-quarter cheese. Top with second tortilla. Lightly butter top of quesadilla. 10. Cook them for 3 minutes. 11. Transfer cooked quesadilla to a large plate and repeat with remaining three quesadillas. Slice each quesadilla into six sections. 12. Serve warm.
Per Serving: Calories 838; Fat 48.84g; Sodium 1655mg; Carbs 59.72gg; Fibre 4.3g; Sugar 5.57g; Protein 42.29g

Chili Beef Bean Pie

Prep Time: 15 minutes | **Cook Time:** 11 minutes | **Serves:** 4

2 teaspoons olive oil
225g beef mince
½ small yellow onion, peeled and diced
1 small carrot, peeled and diced
1 medium celery stalk, diced
1 (450g) can chili beans in chili sauce
115g canned fire-roasted diced tomatoes, drained
½ teaspoon ground cumin
½ teaspoon chili powder
¼ teaspoon salt
45g corn chips
50g grated cheese blend

1. Heat oil for 30 seconds in a large skillet over medium-high heat; add beef, onion, carrot, and celery, and cook them for 5 minutes until beef is no longer pink. Drain fat from pan. 2. Stir in beans including sauce, diced tomatoes, cumin, chili powder, and salt. Remove from heat. 3. Preheat air fryer at 175°C for 3 minutes. 4. Spoon beef mixture in a suitable cake barrel. Evenly distribute corn chips on top, followed by cheese. 5. Place pan in air fryer basket, and cook for 6 minutes. 6. Remove pan from air fryer and let rest 10 minutes. Serve warm.
Per Serving: Calories 491; Fat 13.37g; Sodium 2105mg; Carbs 60.52g; Fibre 11.8g; Sugar 15.88g; Protein 29.32g

Tacos with Pickled Radishes

Prep Time: 5 minutes | **Cook Time:** 20 minutes | **Serves:** 10 tacos

For Quick Pickled Radishes
5 medium radishes, julienned
2 tablespoons white wine vinegar
½ teaspoon granulated sugar
⅛ teaspoon salt
For Tacos
60ml olive oil
½ teaspoon salt
½ teaspoon ground cumin
1 (454g) flank steak
10 (10cm) mini gluten-free flour tortillas
70g shredded red cabbage

1. To make the pickled radishes, combine Quick Pickled Radishes ingredients in a small bowl, then cover the bowl and refrigerate them until ready to use. 2. To make tacos, combine olive oil, salt, and cumin in a large bowl; add the flank steak and toss, then cover the bowl and refrigerate them for 30 minutes. 3. Preheat the air fryer at 160°C for 3 minutes. 4. Place steak in the air fryer basket and cook 10 minutes. 4. Flip steak, then cook an additional 9 minutes until medium rare. 5. Transfer steak to a large cutting board and let rest 5 minutes. Slice thinly against the grain. 6. Build tacos by adding steak slices to flour tortillas along with red cabbage and pickled radishes. Serve immediately.
Per Serving: Calories 428; Fat 18.13g; Sodium 987mg; Carbs 49.95g; Fibre 2.8g; Sugar 4.16g; Protein 15.2g

Pork-Beef Meatballs

Prep Time: 10 minutes | **Cook Time:** 16 minutes | **Serves:** 6

1 slice gluten-free sandwich bread, torn into bite-sized pieces
2 tablespoons whole milk
225g beef mince
225g pork mince
1 large egg
2 tablespoons finely diced peeled yellow onion
1 teaspoon minced seeded habanero
1 teaspoon Jamaican jerk seasoning
½ lime

1. Preheat the air fryer at 175°C for 3 minutes. Lightly grease the air fryer basket with cooking oil. 2. Add bread to a large bowl with milk and toss, add remaining ingredients except lime. 3. Squeeze ingredients together until fully combined, then form mixture into eighteen meatballs, about 2 tablespoons each. 4. Add half of meatballs to air fryer basket, and cook them for 6 minutes. 5. Flip meatballs, and cook them for an additional 2 minutes. 6. Transfer the cooked meatballs to a large serving dish. You can cook the meatballs in batches. 7. Squeeze lime over meatballs and serve.
Per Serving: Calories 194; Fat 11.06g; Sodium 92mg; Carbs 4.36g; Fibre 0.2g; Sugar 3.06g; Protein 18.59g

Steak Salad

Prep Time: 5 minutes | **Cook Time:** 20 minutes | **Serves:** 4

60ml olive oil
1 teaspoon + ⅛ teaspoon salt, divided
½ teaspoon + ⅛ teaspoon ground black pepper, divided
1 (450g) flank steak
60ml balsamic vinaigrette
1 tablespoon Dijon mustard
160g rocket
4 tablespoons crumbled blue cheese
½ medium red onion, peeled and cut into thin strips
4 tablespoons pecan pieces
4 tablespoons sunflower seeds
280g sliced hulled strawberries

1. Combine the olive oil, 1 teaspoon salt, and ½ teaspoon pepper in a gallon-sized plastic resealable bag. Add flank steak and toss, then refrigerate them for 30 minutes up to overnight. 2. Preheat the air fryer at 160°C for 3 minutes. Lightly grease the air fryer basket with cooking oil. 3. Place steak in air fryer basket, and cook 10 minutes. 4. Flip steak and cook for an additional 9 minutes until medium rare. 5. Transfer the steak to a cutting board, and let rest 5 minutes, then slice thinly across the grain. 6. While steak is resting, Whisk balsamic vinaigrette with Dijon mustard in a large bowl. Add rocket and season with remaining salt and pepper. Toss, then divide into four serving bowls. 7. Top each salad with blue cheese, red onion, pecans, sunflower seeds, strawberries, and sliced steak. Serve immediately.
Per Serving: Calories 35; Fat 29.12g; Sodium 393mg; Carbs 10.35g; Fibre 3.5g; Sugar 4.82g; Protein 15.93g

Worcestershire Pork Tenderloin

Prep time: 10 minutes| **Cook time:** 16 minutes| **Serves:** 2

1 tablespoon smoked paprika
2 teaspoons ground cumin
1 teaspoon garlic powder
1 teaspoon onion powder
¼ teaspoon cayenne pepper
1 teaspoon salt
½ teaspoon freshly ground black pepper
1 teaspoon Italian seasoning
2 tablespoons butter, melted
1 teaspoon Worcestershire sauce
1 (450g) pork tenderloin, halved crosswise

1. Combine the paprika, cumin, garlic powder, onion powder, cayenne pepper, salt, black pepper, and Italian seasoning in a small bowl. Set aside. 2. Heat your air fryer at 350°F/ 175°C for 3 minutes in advance. 3. Whisk together the butter and Worcestershire sauce in a separate small bowl. Brush over the pork tenderloin halves, then rub with seasoning mix. 4. Place the pork in an air fryer basket lightly greased with olive oil and cook for 8 minutes, then flip. Cook an additional 8 minutes, then, using a meat thermometer, ensure the internal temperature is at least 140°F/ 60°C. 5. Let the pork tenderloin rest for 5 minutes before slicing and serving warm on a cutting board.
Per Serving: Calories 376; Fat 18g; Sodium 1489mg; Carbs 6.7g; Fibre 2g; Sugar 1g; Protein 45g

Citrusy Pork Ribs

Prep time: 10 minutes| **Cook time:** 40 minutes| **Serves:** 4

60ml water
1 teaspoon smoked paprika
1 teaspoon ground cumin
1 teaspoon garlic powder
1 tablespoon Swerve brown sugar
½ teaspoon ground mustard
1 teaspoon salt
½ teaspoon freshly ground black pepper
2 tablespoons olive oil
1 tablespoon fresh orange juice
900g country-style pork ribs

1. Heat the air fryer at 350°F/ 175°C for 3 minutes in advance. Pour water into the bottom of your air fryer to ensure minimum smoke from fat drippings. 2. Combine the paprika, cumin, garlic powder, brown sugar, ground mustard, salt, and pepper in a small bowl, then set it aside. 3. Whisk together the olive oil and orange juice in a separate small bowl and massage it into the pork ribs. Season the ribs with the spice mixture. 4. Add the pork to an ungreased air fryer basket. Cook in your air fryer for 40 minutes, flipping every 10 minutes. 5. Transfer the pork to a large serving plate and serve warm.
Per Serving: Calories 399; Fat 20g; Sodium 736mg; Carbs 5g; Fibre 0g; Sugar 3.5g; Protein 47.5g

Tex-Mex Andouille Sausage

Prep Time: 10 minutes | **Cook Time:** 20 minutes | **Serves:** 4

1 tablespoon olive oil
40g finely diced peeled yellow onion
1 medium green pepper, seeded and diced
480g cooked wild rice
165g canned corn, drained
55g mayonnaise
2 tablespoons sour cream
60g crumbled feta cheese
1 teaspoon chili powder
1 teaspoon salt
1 teaspoon ground black pepper
175g cooked andouille sausage, cut into 2 cm sections

1. Heat the olive oil in a medium skillet over medium-high heat for 30 seconds; add onion and pepper, and cook them for 4 minutes until onions are translucent. Remove the skillet from heat. 2. Combine wild rice, corn, mayonnaise, sour cream, feta cheese, chili powder, salt, and black pepper in a large bowl. Stir in onion and pepper mixture, and the sausage. 3. Preheat the air fryer at 175°C for 3 minutes. 4. Transfer sausage and rice mixture to a suitable cake tin lightly greased with preferred cooking oil, then place in the air fryer basket. 5. Cook the food in the air fryer for 15 minutes. 6. Let the food rest for 10 minutes after cooking. Serve warm.
Per Serving: Calories 523; Fat 22.14g; Sodium 1239mg; Carbs 65.6g; Fibre 7.5g; Sugar 2.41g; Protein 20.69g

Pork Bratwurst and Sauerkraut

Prep Time: 10 minutes | **Cook Time:** 21 minutes | **Serves:** 5

455g uncooked pork bratwurst, approximately 5 links, pierced with a fork
1 (350ml) gluten-free bottle lager beer
480ml water
½ medium yellow onion, peeled and sliced
450g drained sauerkraut
2 tablespoons German mustard

1. Add bratwurst to a medium saucepan with beer, water, and onion. Bring to a boil over high heat. Reduce heat to medium and simmer 15 minutes. Drain. 2. Preheat the air fryer at 200°C for 3 minutes. Lightly grease the air fryer basket with cooking oil. 3. Place bratwurst and onions in air fryer basket, and cook them for 6 minutes. flipping bratwurst and adding sauerkraut halfway through cooking. Use a meat thermometer to ensure internal temperature of bratwurst is at least 70°C. 4. Transfer bratwurst, onions, and sauerkraut to a large plate and serve warm with mustard on the side.
Per Serving: Calories 158; Fat 5.38g; Sodium 1523mg; Carbs 11.58g; Fibre 2.2g; Sugar 2.73g; Protein 16.94g

Miso-Glazed Pork Loin Roast

Prep Time: 10 minutes | **Cook Time:** 40 minutes | **Serves:** 6

3 tablespoons red miso paste
2 tablespoons honey
1 tablespoon sesame oil
¼ teaspoon ground ginger
2 cloves garlic, peeled and minced
½ teaspoon salt
½ teaspoon ground white pepper
1 (900g) boneless pork loin

1. Preheat air fryer at 175°C for 3 minutes. Lightly grease the air fryer basket with cooking oil. 2. Whisk together miso, honey, sesame oil, ground ginger, garlic, salt, and pepper in a small bowl. 3. Massage mixture into all sides of pork loin. 4. Place pork in air fryer basket, and cook the pork for 40 minutes until it reaches an internal temperature of at least 60°C, flipping the pork halfway though. 5. Transfer the pork to a cutting board to rest 5 minutes before slicing and serving warm.
Per Serving: Calories 312; Fat 15.39g; Sodium 582mg; Carbs 8.76g; Fibre 0.6g; Sugar 6.48g; Protein 33.43g

Cherry Pork Chops

Prep Time: 5 minutes | **Cook Time:** 12 minutes | **Serves:** 2

2 tablespoons cherry preserves
1 tablespoon ketchup
1 tablespoon Dijon mustard
2 teaspoons light brown sugar
1 teaspoon Worcestershire sauce
1 tablespoon lime juice
1 tablespoon olive oil
2 cloves garlic, peeled and minced
2 (250g) bone-in pork chops, 2cm thick

1. Whisk together cherry preserves, ketchup, Dijon mustard, brown sugar, Worcestershire sauce, lime juice, olive oil, and garlic in a medium bowl; add pork chops to mixture and toss. 2. Cover the bowl and refrigerate them for 30 minutes. 3. Preheat the air fryer at 175°C for 3 minutes. Lightly grease the air fryer basket with cooking oil. 4. Place pork chops in air fryer basket, and cook them for 4 minutes. 5. Flip chops, cook 4 minutes, then flip them once more and cook for an additional 4 minutes until they have an internal temperature of at least 60°C. 6. Transfer pork to a cutting board to rest 5 minutes before serving warm.
Per Serving: Calories 401; Fat 22.73g; Sodium 272mg; Carbs 10.84g; Fibre 0.6g; Sugar 7.95g; Protein 37.03g

Orange Pork over Rice

Prep Time: 10 minutes | **Cook Time:** 17 minutes | **Serves:** 4

120ml freshly squeezed orange juice
2 tablespoons orange marmalade
1 tablespoon avocado oil
1 tablespoon tamari
2 teaspoons sriracha
1 teaspoon yellow mustard
1 (450g) pork shoulder, trimmed and thinly sliced into 2cm strips
2 tablespoons water
665g cooked white rice
15g chopped fresh coriander

1. Whisk the orange juice, orange marmalade, oil, tamari, sriracha, and yellow mustard in a medium bowl. Set aside half of marinade. 2. Add pork strips to bowl with half of marinade and toss, cover the bowl and refrigerate them for 30 minutes. 3. Preheat the air fryer at 175°C for 3 minutes. 4. Add water to bottom of air fryer. Add pork to the air fryer basket, and cook for 5 minutes. 5. Toss them, and cook for 6 minutes, then toss once more and cook for an additional 6 minutes. 6. Transfer pork to a medium bowl and toss with remaining marinade. 7. Serve over cooked rice and garnish with fresh coriander.
Per Serving: Calories 599; Fat 24.02g; Sodium 351mg; Carbs 58.47g; Fibre 0.3g; Sugar 3.44g; Protein 33.67g

Roasted Dijon Pork Loin

Prep time: 10 minutes| **Cook time:** 40 minutes| **Serves:** 4

2 tablespoons Dijon mustard
2 teaspoons olive oil
½ teaspoon salt
¼ teaspoon freshly ground black pepper
1 teaspoon dried rosemary
1 (900g) boneless pork loin roast

1. Heat your air fryer at 350°F/ 175°C for 3 minutes in advance. 2. In a small bowl, whisk together the mustard, olive oil, salt, pepper, and rosemary. Massage into loin on all sides. 3. Place the pork in an ungreased air fryer basket. Cook for 20 minutes. Flip and cook for an additional 20 minutes. Using a meat thermometer, ensure an internal temperature is at least 145°F/ 60°C. 4. Let the pork loin rest on a cutting board for 5 minutes before slicing and serving warm.
Per Serving: Calories 325; Fat 11.7g; Sodium 488mg; Carbs 0g; Fibre 0g; Sugar 0g; Protein 51g

Pork Bratwursts and Sauerkraut

Prep time: 10 minutes| **Cook time:** 21 minutes| **Serves:** 4

450g (5 links) uncooked pork bratwurst, each piece pierced with a fork twice
480ml beef broth
480ml water
½ medium yellow onion, peeled and sliced into half-moons
300g drained sauerkraut
2 tablespoons German mustard

1. Add the bratwurst, beef broth, water, and onion to a medium saucepan. Bring them together to a boil over high heat, then reduce the heat to low and simmer for 15 minutes, then drain. 2. Heat your air fryer at 400°F/ 200°C for 3 minutes in advance. 3. Place the bratwursts and onion in an ungreased air fryer basket. Cook for 3 minutes. Flip the bratwursts, add sauerkraut, and cook for an additional 3 minutes. Using a meat thermometer, ensure the internal temperature is at least 160°F/ 70°C. 4. Transfer the bratwursts, onion, and sauerkraut to a large serving plate and serve warm with mustard on the side.
Per Serving: Calories 278; Fat 12g; Sodium 2357mg; Carbs 17g; Fibre 3g; Sugar 5.5g; Protein 26g

Stuffed Pork Loins with Mushrooms

Prep time: 10 minutes| **Cook time:** 17 minutes| **Serves:** 3

2 teaspoons olive oil
½ medium yellow onion, peeled and diced
50g diced white mushrooms
½ teaspoon salt
½ teaspoon freshly ground black pepper
3 (450g, approximately 2cm-thick) boneless centre-cut pork loins, a pocket cut into each
6 thin slices Swiss cheese

1. Set the heat to medium-high and heat the olive oil for 2 minutes in a medium skillet. Add onion and mushrooms and stir-fry for 3 minutes until the onion is translucent. Add salt and pepper. Continue to cook for an additional minute. 2. Heat your air fryer at 350°F/ 175°C for 3 minutes in advance. 3. Stuff an even amount of mushroom mixture into each pork chop pocket. Put 2 Swiss cheese slices into each pocket. 4. Place pork in the air fryer basket lightly greased with olive oil. Cook for 11 minutes. Using a meat thermometer, ensure an internal temperature is at least 145°F/ 60°C. 5. Let the pork loins rest on a cutting board for 5 minutes before serving warm.
Per Serving: Calories 899; Fat 33.5g; Sodium 761mg; Carbs 4.7g; Fibre 0g; Sugar 1.7g; Protein 136g

Delicious Cereal-Crusted Pork Chops

Prep Time: 5 minutes | **Cook Time:** 12 minutes | **Serves:** 2

1 large egg
1 tablespoon Dijon mustard
25g grated Parmesan cheese
15g crushed gluten-free bran cereal
¼ teaspoon ground black pepper
2 (220g) bone-in pork chops, 2 cm thick

1. Preheat the air fryer at 175°C for 3 minutes. Lightly grease the air fryer basket with cooking oil. 2. Whisk egg and Dijon mustard in a small dish, and in a separate shallow dish, combine the Parmesan cheese, bran cereal, and black pepper. 3. Dip pork chops in egg mixture, then dredge in cereal mixture. 4. Place the pork chops in air fryer basket, and cook for 4 minutes. 5. Flip pork and cook them for 4 minutes, then flip once more and cook an additional 4 minutes until they have an internal temperature of at least 60°C. 6. Transfer pork to a cutting board and let rest for 5 minutes before serving warm.
Per Serving: Calories 338; Fat 18.64g; Sodium 401mg; Carbs 6.12g; Fibre 0.5g; Sugar 0.56g; Protein 34.64g

Vegetable-Stuffed Pork Loins

Prep Time: 5 minutes | **Cook Time:** 18 minutes | **Serves:** 3

3 slices uncooked bacon, diced
½ medium yellow onion, peeled and diced
35g diced white mushrooms
30g baby spinach
½ teaspoon salt
½ teaspoon ground black pepper
90g cooked quinoa
3 (455g) boneless centre-cut pork loins, 2cm thick, pocket cut in each loin

1. Cook bacon in a medium skillet over medium-high heat for 3 minutes until fat is rendered but not crispy. 2. Add onion and mushrooms to skillet, and stir-fry for 3 minutes until onions are translucent; add spinach, salt, and pepper, and continue to cook another 1 minute until spinach is wilted. 3. Remove skillet from heat, and add the quinoa and combine them well. 4. Preheat the air fryer at 175°C for 3 minutes. Lightly grease the air fryer basket with cooking oil. 5. Stuff quinoa mixture into each pork loin and place pork in air fryer basket, and cook 11 minutes until they have an internal temperature of at least 60°C. 6. Transfer pork to a cutting board and let them rest for 5 minutes before slicing and serving warm.
Per Serving: Calories 362; Fat 18.28g; Sodium 611mg; Carbs 10.09g; Fibre 1.7g; Sugar 2g; Protein 37.8g

Fried Hangover Sandwiches

Prep Time: 10 minutes | **Cook Time:** 20 minutes | **Serves:** 2

½ (340g) can SPAM, cut into 4 slices
4 teaspoons yellow mustard
4 slices gluten-free sandwich bread
8 slices deli ham
8 dill pickle chips
2 slices Swiss cheese
4 tablespoons butter, melted

1. Preheat the air fryer at 190°C for 3 minutes. Lightly grease the air fryer basket with cooking oil. 2. Place SPAM slices in air fryer basket, and cook them for 6 minutes, flipping them halfway through. Transfer them to a medium plate after cooking. 3. Adjust the air fryer temperature to 175°C. 4. Assemble sandwiches by spreading 1 teaspoon mustard to each bread slice. Layer bottom bread slice with portioned SPAM, ham, dill pickle chips, and Swiss cheese. Place top bread slices on toppings. 5. Brush outside top and bottom of each sandwich with melted butter. 6. Place one sandwich in the air fryer basket, and cook for 6 minutes, flipping it halfway through. Repeat with remaining sandwich. 7. Serve warm.
Per Serving: Calories 783; Fat 46.67g; Sodium 1767mg; Carbs 38.53g; Fibre 9.6g; Sugar 9.56g; Protein 54.68g

Pork Meatballs

Prep Time: 15 minutes | **Cook Time:** 16 minutes | **Serves:** 4

455g pork mince
1 large egg
1 tablespoon gochujang
1 teaspoon tamari
¼ teaspoon ground ginger
30g plain gluten-free bread crumbs
1 spring onion, whites minced, greens sliced, divided
4 tablespoons orange marmalade

1. Preheat air fryer at 175°C for 3 minutes. Lightly grease the air fryer basket with cooking oil. 2. Combine pork, egg, gochujang, tamari, ginger, bread crumbs, and minced spring onion whites in a large bowl. Form the mixture into sixteen meatballs. 3. Add eight meatballs to air fryer basket and cook them for 6 minutes. 4. Flip meatballs. Cook an additional 2 minutes. Transfer to a large plate. Do the same with the remaining meatballs. 5. Garnish the meatballs with sliced spring onion greens and marmalade, and then serve warm.
Per Serving: Calories 333; Fat 25.33g; Sodium 208mg; Carbs 3.72g; Fibre 0.3g; Sugar 1.76g; Protein 21.32g

Pork Cabbage Salad

Prep Time: 10 minutes | **Cook Time:** 17 minutes | **Serves:** 4

For Crema
60g sour cream
60g mayonnaise
1 tablespoon lime juice
½ teaspoon salt

For Pork Marinade
1 tablespoon sesame oil
1 tablespoon tamari
2 teaspoons sriracha
2 teaspoons honey
1 (2cm) knob fresh ginger, peeled and minced
1 (455g) pork shoulder, trimmed and thinly sliced into 2cm thick strips

For Salad
4 medium radishes, julienned
1 medium shallot, peeled and thinly sliced
3 tablespoons rice vinegar
⅛ teaspoon salt
2 tablespoons water
2 medium carrots, peeled and shaved into long ribbons
270g shredded napa cabbage
5g chopped fresh basil leaves
5g chopped fresh mint leaves

1. To make the crema, whisk the Crema ingredients in a small bowl, then cover the bowl and refrigerate them until ready to use. 2. To make the pork marinade, whisk sesame oil, tamari, sriracha, honey, and minced ginger in a medium bowl. Set aside half of marinade in another medium bowl. 3. Add pork strips to bowl with remaining marinade and toss. Cover the bowl and refrigerate until ready to use. 4. To make the salad, add radishes, shallot, rice vinegar, and salt to a serving bowl, then cover the bowl and refrigerate them until ready to use. 5. Preheat the air fryer at 175°C for 3 minutes. 6. Add water to bottom of air fryer. Add pork to the air fryer basket. 7. Cook the pork for 5 minutes. Toss and resume cooking for 6 minutes. Then, toss once more and cook for an additional 6 minutes. 8. Transfer pork to bowl with reserved marinade and toss. 9. Add carrots to the air fryer basket and cook for 2 minutes. 10. Distribute cabbage, basil, and mint to four serving bowls. Top with pork, carrots, and radish mixture. Drizzle Crema over top and serve.
Per Serving: Calories 292; Fat 16.22g; Sodium 875mg; Carbs 11.37g; Fibre 1.3g; Sugar 5.09g; Protein 24.82g

Chimichurri Flank Steak

Prep Time: 5 minutes | **Cook Time:** 20 minutes | **Serves:** 4

For Marinade
160ml olive oil
Juice of 1 medium orange
1 teaspoon orange zest
Juice of 1 lime
1 teaspoon lime zest
80ml tamari sauce
2 tablespoons red wine vinegar
4 cloves garlic, peeled and minced
1 (450g) flank steak

For Chimichurri Sauce
60g fresh Italian parsley leaves
15g fresh coriander leaves
15g fresh oregano leaves
60ml olive oil
½ small yellow onion, peeled and diced
4 cloves garlic, peeled and minced
2 tablespoons lime juice
2 teaspoons lime zest
2 tablespoons red wine vinegar
⅛ teaspoon cayenne pepper
½ teaspoon ground cumin
½ teaspoon salt

1. To make the marinade, combine the olive oil, orange juice, orange zest, lime juice, lime zest, tamari sauce, red wine vinegar, and garlic in a plastic resealable bag. 2. Add flank steak and toss. Refrigerate them for 1 hour up to overnight. 3. To make the Chimichurri sauce, place all the Chimichurri Sauce ingredients in a food processor or blender, then pulse them several times until desired consistency. 4. Cover the sauce and refrigerate until ready to use. 5. Preheat the air fryer at 160°C for 3 minutes. Lightly grease the air fryer basket with cooking oil. 6. Place steak in air fryer basket, and cook 10 minutes. 7. Flip steak and cook an additional 9 minutes until medium rare. 8. Transfer steak to a cutting board. Let rest 5 minutes, then slice thinly against the grain. 9. Serve the steak with Chimichurri Sauce.

Per Serving: Calories 551; Fat 52.16g; Sodium 1654mg; Carbs 9.62g; Fibre 1.2g; Sugar 3.28g; Protein 13.03g

Mustard Pork over Cauliflower Rice

Prep time: 15 minutes| **Cook time:** 25 minutes| **Serves:** 4

For Pork
2 tablespoons avocado oil
2 tablespoons coconut aminos
2 teaspoons red chilli paste
5g sweetener
1 (450g) pork shoulder, trimmed
2 tablespoons water
2 teaspoons yellow mustard

For Cauliflower Rice
1 tablespoon coconut oil
320g cauliflower rice
6 scallions, whites and greens separated, divided
4 cloves garlic, peeled and minced
250ml canned unsweetened coconut milk
1 tablespoon fresh lime juice
1 teaspoon lime zest
½ teaspoon salt

To make Pork: 1. Trim the pork shoulder and then thinly slice the meat into 2cm strips. Whisk together avocado oil, coconut aminos, mustard, red chilli paste, and sweetener in a medium bowl. Set aside half of marinade. 2. Add the pork strips to a bowl with the remaining marinade and toss. Cover the pork and refrigerate for 30 minutes. 3. Heat your air fryer at 350°F/ 175°C for 3 minutes before cooking. To ensure minimum smoke from fat drippings, pour water into the bottom of the air fryer. 4. Add the pork to your ungreased air fryer basket. Cook for 7 minutes. Toss. Cook for an additional 10 minutes. 5. Transfer the pork to a bowl with the remaining marinade and toss well, then set aside.
To make Cauliflower Rice: 1. Heat the coconut oil over medium-high heat for 30 seconds in a large skillet. Add the cauliflower rice, scallion whites, and garlic. Toss well, then place a lid on the skillet, reduce the heat to low, and let steam for 2 minutes. 2. Uncover the skillet and then stir in the lime juice, lime zest, coconut milk, and salt. Let them cook uncovered for an additional 5 minutes until heated through.
Serve the pork over cauliflower rice and garnish with scallion greens.
Per Serving: Calories 475; Fat 33.3g; Sodium 487mg; Carbs 10.7g; Fibre 2.5g; Sugar 5.6g; Protein 33.4g

Moo Shu Pork with Lettuce

Prep Time: 15 minutes | **Cook Time:** 25 minutes | **Serves:** 4

3 tablespoons cornflour, divided
1 tablespoon water
2 tablespoons rice vinegar
3 tablespoons gluten-free hoisin sauce
1 teaspoon oyster sauce
1 teaspoon + 1 tablespoon sesame oil, divided
¼ teaspoon ground ginger
1 large egg
2 tablespoons gluten-free plain flour
1 (455g) boneless pork loin, cut into 2 cm cubes
1 (400g) bag coleslaw mix
3 medium green onions, sliced
50g sliced shiitake mushrooms
8 iceberg lettuce leaves

1. Whisk 1 tablespoon cornflour and water in a small bowl. Set aside. 2. Add rice vinegar, hoisin sauce, oyster sauce, 1 teaspoon sesame oil, and ground ginger to a small saucepan, and cook them over medium heat for 3 minutes, stirring continuously. 3. Add cornflour slurry, and cook for another 1 minute. Set aside to allow mixture to thicken. 4. In a medium bowl, whisk the egg, flour, and remaining cornflour in a medium bowl. Set aside. 5. Preheat the air fryer at 175°C for 3 minutes. Lightly grease the air fryer basket with cooking oil. 6. Dredge pork cubes in egg mixture. Shake off any excess. 7. Add half of pork to air fryer basket, and cook them for 8 minutes until they have an internal temperature of at least 60°C, shaking the basket gently halfway through. 8. Do the same with the remaining food. 9. While pork is cooking, add the remaining sesame oil to a large skillet; add coleslaw mix, green onions, and mushrooms, and cook them for 5 minutes over medium heat until coleslaw is wilted. Remove the skillet from heat. 10. Transfer cooked pork to skillet with cooked coleslaw mix. Add sauce and toss until coated. 11. Serve warm wrapped in lettuce leaves.

Per Serving: Calories 271; Fat 9.24g; Sodium 217mg; Carbs 18.5g; Fibre 0.7g; Sugar 3.25g; Protein 26.96g

Dessert Recipes

Peanut Butter Cookies

Prep Time: 10 minutes | **Cook Time:** 8 minutes | **Serves:** 9

35g almond flour
5g sweetener
1 large egg
½ teaspoon vanilla extract
4 tablespoons butter, melted
⅛ teaspoon salt
4 tablespoons powdered peanut butter

1. Preheat air fryer at 175°C for 3 minutes. Grease the pizza pan with cooking spray. 2. Combine all ingredients in a medium bowl. 3. Spoon mixture into the pizza pan greased, and place pan in air fryer basket. 4. Cook the cookie for 8 minutes. 5. Slice the cookie and serve warm.
Per Serving: Calories 99; Fat 8.68g; Sodium 120mg; Carbs 4.36g; Fibre 1.1g; Sugar 0.83g; Protein 2.87g

Orange Glazed Strawberry Cake

Prep Time: 10 minutes | **Cook Time:** 10 minutes | **Serves:** 4

For Cake
50g finely ground almond flour
5g sweetener
½ teaspoon baking powder
⅛ teaspoon salt
2 tablespoons butter, melted
1 large egg
2 teaspoons orange zest
½ teaspoon unflavoured gelatin
½ teaspoon vanilla extract
½ teaspoon ground cinnamon
40g hulled and finely chopped strawberries
For Glaze
1 tablespoon butter, melted
¼ teaspoon orange zest
1 tablespoon orange juice
5g sweetener

1. Preheat air fryer at 150°C for 3 minutes. 2. Combine the flour, sweetener, baking powder, and salt in a large bowl. 3. Combine butter, egg, orange zest, gelatin, vanilla, cinnamon, strawberries in a small bowl, then add them to flour mixture, and stir until combined. 4. Spoon mixture into an ungreased pizza pan, and place the pan in air fryer basket. 5. Cook the mixture for 10 minutes. Remove pan from basket and let set for about 30 minutes until cooled. 6. Combine butter, orange zest, orange juice, and sweetener in a small bowl. Add a little water if glaze is too thick and a little extra sweetener if glaze is too thin. Pour over cooled cake. 6. Slice cake and serve.
Per Serving: Calories 120; Fat 10.4g; Sodium 146mg; Carbs 8.59g; Fibre 3.6g; Sugar 1.42g; Protein 3.85g

Blueberry Jars with Crumble Topping

Prep Time: 10 minutes | **Cook Time:** 24 minutes | **Serves:** 6

For Blueberry Filling
550g fresh blueberries
2 tablespoons almond flour
1 tablespoon pulp-free orange juice
2 teaspoons orange zest
5g sweetener
1 tablespoon butter, melted
⅛ teaspoon salt
6 (100g) oven-safe glass jelly jars
For Crumble Topping
2 tablespoons almond flour
4g sweetener
4 tablespoons pecan pieces
2 tablespoons slivered almonds
2 tablespoons unsweetened coconut flakes
2 tablespoons unsalted sunflower seeds
3 tablespoons butter, melted

1. Preheat air fryer at 175°C for 3 minutes. 2. Combine all ingredients in a large bowl, and then evenly distribute into jelly jars. 3. Place three jars in air fryer basket, and cook them for 7 minutes. Repeat cooking with remaining jars. When jars are removed from air fryer, use the back of a spoon to gently press down on the blueberry filling. Set aside. 4. Combine all ingredients in a medium bowl. Distribute mixture over cooked filling in jars. 5. Place three jars back in air fryer and cook for an additional 5 minutes. Repeat cooking with remaining jars. 6. Let jars cool for 10 minutes before eating or covering. Refrigerate them for up to 4 days until ready to serve.
Per Serving: Calories 285; Fat 18.28g; Sodium 382mg; Carbs 28.1g; Fibre 3g; Sugar 18.94g; Protein 6.26g

Dark Chocolate Custard

Prep Time: 15 minutes | **Cook Time:** 24 minutes | **Serves:** 4

4 large egg yolks
2 tablespoons sweetener
⅛ teaspoon salt
⅛ teaspoon vanilla extract
360g heavy cream
125g sugar-free dark chocolate chips
1 teaspoon ground cinnamon

1. Whisk egg yolks, sweetener, salt, and vanilla in a small bowl. 2. Heat the heavy cream in a medium saucepan over medium-low heat for 4 minutes to a low simmer. 3. Whisk a spoonful of heavy cream into egg mixture to temper eggs, then slowly whisk egg mixture into saucepan with remaining heavy cream. Add chocolate chips and cinnamon and continually stir for 10 minutes on simmer until chocolate is melted. 4. Remove pan from heat and evenly distribute chocolate mixture among four ungreased custard ramekins. 5. Preheat the air fryer at 175°C for 3 minutes. 6. Place two ramekins in air fryer basket. Cook them for 7 minutes. Transfer ramekins to a cooling rack. Repeat cooking with remaining two ramekins. 7. Allow ramekins to cool for 15 minutes, then refrigerate covered at least 2 hours before serving.
Per Serving: Calories 308; Fat 23.86g; Sodium 191mg; Carbs 19.33g; Fibre 1g; Sugar 10.87g; Protein 4.86g

Lemony Kiwi Pavlova

Prep time: 15 minutes| **Cook time:** 90 minutes| **Serves:** 2

For Pavlova
2 egg whites
¼ teaspoon cornflour
½ cup granulated sugar
½ teaspoon lemon juice
½ teaspoon vanilla extract

For Topping
80ml double cream
1 teaspoon lemon juice
¼ teaspoon lemon zest
2 tablespoons granulated sugar
2 medium kiwis, peeled and sliced

To make Pavlova: 1. Cut a sheet of parchment to the size of a grill pan. Then draw a 15cm circle on the paper. Flip the paper, ink side down, onto the grill pan. You should be able to see a circle outline through paper. Set aside. 2. In a large metal bowl, set an electric mixer to high speed and beat egg whites. Still beating, add cornflour. Then add sugar, 1 tablespoon at a time until stiff peaks form in the mixture. Add lemon juice and vanilla. 3. Preheat your air fryer at 225°F/ 105°C for 5 minutes. 4. Spoon or pipe the egg white mixture over the parchment paper circle, creating higher edges around the perimeter (like a short pie crust). There should be an indention in the centre. Add the grill pan to an air fryer basket and cook for 60 minutes. 5. Once done, turn off the heat and leave the grill pan with pavlova in the air fryer for an additional 30 minutes. 6. Remove the grill pan from the air fryer and gently peel off the parchment paper from the bottom of the pavlova. Transfer pavlova to a large plate.
To make Topping: Whisk together the double cream, lemon juice, lemon zest, and sugar in a medium bowl until creamy.
Fill the pavlova 'crust' with whipped cream mixture and top with kiwi slices. Serve.
Per Serving: Calories 261; Fat 8g; Sodium 65mg; Carbs 45g; Fibre 2g; Sugar 40g; Protein 5g

Coco Rum Custard

Prep Time: 15 minutes | **Cook Time:** 20 minutes | **Serves:** 4

4 large egg yolks
5 g sweetener
1 teaspoon rum extract
⅛ teaspoon salt
1 (380g) can sugar-free coconut cream
60g heavy cream

1. Whisk egg yolks, sweetener, rum extract, and salt in a small bowl. Set aside.
2. Heat coconut cream and heavy cream in a medium saucepan over medium-low heat for 5 minutes to a low simmer. 3. Whisk a spoonful heated cream mixture into egg mixture to temper eggs, then slowly whisk egg mixture into a saucepan with remaining heavy cream. 4. Remove pan from heat and evenly distribute mixture among four ungreased custard ramekins. 5. Preheat the air fryer at 175°C for 3 minutes. 6. Place two ramekins in air fryer basket, and cook the food for 7 minutes. Transfer to a cooling rack and repeat cooking with remaining two ramekins. 8. Allow ramekins to cool for 15 minutes, then refrigerate covered at least 2 hours before serving.
Per Serving: Calories 219; Fat 7.99g; Sodium 195mg; Carbs 30.82g; Fibre 8.7g; Sugar 8.97g; Protein 8.04g

Chocolate Cake

Prep Time: 5 minutes | **Cook Time:** 15 minutes | **Serves:** 2

For Cake
65g finely ground almond flour
20g cocoa
10g sweetener
1 teaspoon baking powder
⅛ teaspoon salt
⅛ teaspoon ground cinnamon
⅛ teaspoon chili powder
4 tablespoons butter, melted
2 large eggs
1 teaspoon vanilla extract

For Chocolate Ganache
40g sugar-free chocolate chips
2 tablespoons heavy cream
2g sweetener

1. Preheat air fryer at 175°C for 3 minutes. 2. Combine flour, cocoa, sweetener, baking powder, salt, cinnamon, and chili powder in a large bowl. 3. Mix the butter, eggs, and vanilla in a small bowl, then add them to flour mixture and stir until smooth. 4. Spoon mixture into a cake barrel lightly greased with olive oil. Place barrel in air fryer basket and cook for 11 minutes. 5. Remove barrel from basket and let set for about 10 minutes until cool. 6. In a double boiler, add all ingredients and place over medium heat. Continuously whisk the mixture for about 4 minutes until smooth. 7. Pour ganache over cooled cake and let set for 30 minutes. Slice and serve.

Per Serving: Calories 518; Fat 43.75g; Sodium 447mg; Carbs 36.09g; Fibre 7.7g; Sugar 1.27g; Protein 9.19g

Cinnamon Chocolate Custard

Prep time: 15 minutes | **Cook time:** 24 minutes | **Serves:** 4

4 large egg yolks
2 tablespoons granulated sugar
⅛ teaspoon salt
⅛ teaspoon almond extract
360ml half cream
125g semi-sweet chocolate chips
1 teaspoon ground cinnamon

1. Whisk together the egg yolks, sugar, salt, and almond extract in a small bowl. When done, set aside. 2. Set a medium saucepan onto medium-low heat and bring half cream to a low simmer. Whisk a spoonful of heated half cream into the egg mixture, then slowly whisk the egg mixture into a saucepan. Add chocolate chips and cinnamon and continually stir for 10 minutes until the chocolate is melted. 3. Preheat your air fryer at 350°F/ 175°C for 3 minutes. 4. Remove the pan from the heat and evenly distribute the chocolate mixture among 4 ungreased ramekins. 5. Place 2 ramekins in the air fryer basket. Cook for 7 minutes. 6. Transfer cooked custards to a cooling rack. Repeat with remaining custards. 7. Allow custards to cool for about 15 minutes, then cover and refrigerate for at least 2 hours before serving, up to 2 days.

Per Serving: Calories 234; Fat 11g; Sodium 243mg; Carbs 28g; Fibre 0g; Sugar 16g; Protein 6g

Lime Almond Cake

Prep Time: 5 minutes | **Cook Time:** 15 minutes | **Serves:** 2

For Cake
100g finely ground almond flour
10g sweetener
1 teaspoon baking powder
½ teaspoon cream of tartar
⅛ teaspoon salt
2 large eggs
125g ricotta cheese
1 tablespoon butter, melted
½ teaspoon vanilla extract
½ teaspoon lime zest
1 tablespoon lime juice

For Topping
1 tablespoon butter, melted
¼ teaspoon lime zest
2 teaspoons lime juice
7g sweetener, divided
2 tablespoons sliced almonds

1. Preheat the air fryer at 150°C for 3 minutes. Grease a suitable spring-form pan with cooking spray. 2. Combine flour, sweetener, baking powder, cream of tartar, and salt in a large bowl; stir in eggs, ricotta cheese, butter, vanilla, lime zest, and lime juice until combined. 3. Spoon mixture into the spring-form pan, then place pan in air fryer basket and cook the mixture for 15 minutes. 4. Remove pan from basket and let cool for 10 minutes, then remove sides of pan. 5. Combine butter, lime zest, lime juice, and 5 g sweetener in a small bowl. Consistency should be a little thicker than a glaze. Spread over top of cooled cake. 6. Garnish with almonds and remaining sweetener. Slice and serve.

Per Serving: Calories 444; Fat 27.1g; Sodium 375mg; Carbs 42.22g; Fibre 4.6g; Sugar 29.31g; Protein 16.4g

Homemade Lemon Curd Palmiers

Prep Time: 15 minutes | **Cook Time:** 25 minutes | **Serves:** 9

3¾ teaspoons sweetener, divided
1 sheet phyllo dough, thawed to room temperature
1 tablespoon butter, melted
95g lemon curd

1. Sprinkle 2 teaspoons of sweetener over a flat and clean surface. 2. Place phyllo sheet over scattered sweetener. Brush butter over sheet. Sprinkle with remaining sweetener. Flip dough. 3. Evenly spread lemon curd over sheet. Carefully roll one end toward the middle of sheet. Stop at the halfway point. Roll opposite side toward the middle, cover and refrigerate for 30 minutes. 4. Slice double log into eighteen equal slices. 5. Preheat air fryer at 175°C for 3 minutes. Lightly grease the air fryer basket with cooking oil. 6. Place six palmiers in air fryer basket. Cook them for 8 minutes. Do the same with the remaining palmiers. 7. Transfer cooked palmiers to a cooling rack. Serve warm or at room temperature.

Per Serving: Calories 25; Fat 1.83g; Sodium 54mg; Carbs 1.82g; Fibre 0.1g; Sugar 0.23g; Protein 0.74g

Chocolate Pavlova with Raspberries

Prep time: 15 minutes| **Cook time:** 90 minutes| **Serves:** 2

For Pavlova
2 large egg whites
¼ teaspoon cornflour
100g granulated sugar
1 tablespoon unsweetened cocoa powder
½ teaspoon apple cider vinegar
½ teaspoon vanilla extract

For Topping
80ml double cream
2 tablespoons granulated sugar
60g fresh raspberries
28g dark chocolate, shaved

To make Pavlova: 1. Cut a sheet of parchment to the size of the grill pan. Draw a 15cm circle on the paper. Flip paper, ink side down, onto the grill pan. You should be able to see a circle outline through paper. Set aside. 2. In a large metal bowl, set an electric mixer to high speed and beat egg whites. Still beating, add cornflour. Add sugar, 1 tablespoon at a time, until stiff peaks form in the mixture. Gently fold in the cocoa powder, apple cider vinegar, and vanilla. 3. Preheat the air fryer at 225°F/ 105°C for 5 minutes. 4. Spoon or pipe egg white mixture over the parchment paper circle, creating higher edges around the perimeter (like a short pie crust). There should be an indention in the centre. 5. Add the grill pan to the air fryer basket and cook for 60 minutes. 6. Once done, turn off the heat and leave the grill pan with the pavlova in the air fryer for an additional 30 minutes. 7. Remove the grill pan from the air fryer and gently peel off the parchment paper from the bottom of the pavlova. Transfer the pavlova to a large plate.

To make Topping: Whisk together the cream and sugar. Fill the pavlova 'crust' with the whipped cream mixture in a medium bowl.

Garnish with raspberries. Sprinkle shaved chocolate over the raspberries and serve.

Per Serving: Calories 385; Fat 13.8g; Sodium 68mg; Carbs 62g; Fibre 4.5g; Sugar 54g; Protein 6g

Amaretto Cheesecake with Almonds

Prep time: 10 minutes| **Cook time:** 22 minutes| **Serves:** 6

For Crust
100g Shreddies
70g blanched slivered almonds
1 tablespoon light brown sugar
3 tablespoons butter, melted

For Cheesecake
400g cream cheese, room temperature
2 tablespoons sour cream
1 large egg
100g granulated sugar
120ml Amaretto liqueur
½ teaspoon lemon juice
⅛ teaspoon salt

To make Crust: 1. Blend the Shreddies, almonds, and brown sugar in a food processor until it has a powdered consistency. Then pour the almond-sugar mixture into a small bowl and add melted butter. Combine with a fork until butter is well distributed. Press mixture into a 18cm springform pan lightly greased with preferred cooking oil. 2. Heat your air fryer at 400°F/200°C for 3 minutes in advance.

To make Cheesecake: 1. Combine cream cheese, sour cream, egg, sugar, Amaretto, lemon juice, and salt in a large bowl. Spoon over the crust. Cover with tin foil. 2. Place the springform pan in an air fryer basket and cook for 16 minutes. Remove tin foil and cook for an additional 6 minutes. 3. Remove cheesecake from the air fryer basket. Cheesecake will be a little jiggly in the centre. Cover and refrigerate for at least 2 hours to allow it to set. Once set, release from the side pan and serve.

Per Serving: Calories 489; Fat 32g; Sodium 398mg; Carbs 36g; Fibre 2g; Sugar 22g; Protein 9g

Strawberry Crumble Jars

Prep Time: 10 minutes | **Cook Time:** 24 minutes | **Serves:** 6

For Filling
500g hulled and small-diced fresh strawberries
2 tablespoons almond flour
2 teaspoons peeled and grated fresh ginger
1 tablespoon lime juice
2 teaspoons lime zest
5g sweetener
1 tablespoon butter, melted
⅛ teaspoon salt
6 (100g) glass jelly jars

For Crumble Topping
2 tablespoons almond flour
2 tablespoons sweetener
1 teaspoon peeled and grated fresh ginger
4 tablespoons pecan pieces
2 tablespoons slivered almonds
2 tablespoons unsweetened coconut flakes
2 tablespoons unsalted sunflower seeds
3 tablespoons butter, melted

1. Preheat the air fryer at 175°C for 3 minutes. 2. Combine strawberries, almond flour, ginger, lime juice, lime zest, sweetener, butter, and salt in a medium bowl. Distribute into jelly jars. 3. Place three jars in air fryer basket, and cook them for 7 minutes. Repeat cooking with remaining jars. 4. When jars are removed from air fryer, use the back of a spoon and gently press down on the strawberry filling. Set aside. 5. Combine all ingredients in a medium bowl, and distribute mixture on top of cooked filling. 6. Add three jars back to air fryer and cook for an additional 5 minutes. Repeat cooking with remaining jars. 7. Let jars cool for 10 minutes before eating or covering. Refrigerate them until ready to serve, up to four days.

Per Serving: Calories 250; Fat 16.36g; Sodium 339mg; Carbs 22.94g; Fibre 2.7g; Sugar 14.74g; Protein 6.39g

Cheesecake with Blackberry Sauce

Prep Time: 10 minutes | **Cook Time:** 30 minutes | **Serves:** 6

For Cheesecake
80g ground walnuts (walnut meal)
3 tablespoons butter, melted
3 tablespoons sweetener
300g cream cheese, room temperature
2 tablespoons sour cream
2 large eggs
5g sweetener
Seeds from 1 vanilla bean
⅛ teaspoon salt

For Blackberry Sauce
220g fresh blackberries
2 tablespoons lemon juice
10g sweetener

1. Preheat the air fryer at 200°C for 3 minutes. 2. Combine ground walnuts, butter, and sweetener in a medium bowl. Press mixture into a suitable spring-form pan. 3. Place pan in air fryer basket and bake for 5 minutes. Remove from basket and allow to cool for at least 30 minutes. 4. Combine cream cheese, sour cream, eggs, sweetener, vanilla bean seeds, and salt in a separate medium bowl. Spoon mixture over cooled crust, then cover with aluminum foil. 5. Place pan back in air fryer basket and cook for 14 minutes. Remove aluminum foil and cook for an additional 5 minutes at 175°C. 6. Transfer them to a bowl and refrigerate for at least 2 hours to allow cheesecake to set. 7. Place ingredients in a small saucepan, and cook over medium heat for 5 minutes. Squash berries against saucepan while cooking. 8. After berries are popped and sauce has thickened, press through a sieve to filter out seeds. 9. Transfer the sauce to a separate bowl, and refrigerate until ready to use. 10. Once cheesecake is cooled and set, release sides of pan, and serve chilled with blackberry sauce on top.

Per Serving: Calories 421; Fat 36.69g; Sodium 770mg; Carbs 11.33g; Fibre 3.9g; Sugar 4.36g; Protein 16.92g

Lime Cheesecake

Prep Time: 10 minutes | **Cook Time:** 20 minutes | **Serves:** 6

80g ground walnuts (walnut meal)
3 tablespoons butter, melted
3 tablespoons sweetener
300g cream cheese, room temperature
2 tablespoons sour cream
2 large eggs
5g sweetener
1 tablespoon key lime zest
1 tablespoon fresh key lime juice
1 teaspoon vanilla extract
⅛ teaspoon salt

1. Preheat the air fryer at 200°C for 3 minutes. 2. Combine ground walnuts, butter, and sweetener in a medium bowl. Press mixture into a suitable spring-form pan. 3. Place the pan in air fryer basket and bake for 5 minutes. Set aside. 4. Combine the cream cheese, sour cream, eggs, sweetener, lime zest, lime juice, vanilla, and salt in a separate medium bowl until smooth, spoon the mixture over cooked crust, then cover them with aluminum foil. 5. Place spring-form pan in air fryer basket and cook for 14 minutes. 6. Remove aluminum foil and cook for an additional 5 minutes at 175°C. Cheesecake will be a little jiggly in the centre when done. 7. Refrigerate the cake at least 2 hours to allow to set. Once set, release sides of pan and serve.

Per Serving: Calories 393; Fat 37.78g; Sodium 452mg; Carbs 7.27g; Fibre 2g; Sugar 2.44g; Protein 10.32g

Conclusion

The air fryer is arguably the most versatile and advanced cooking appliance in the world. These devices have a large capacity and are the perfect cooking companion for you and your family.
The air fryer has numerous cooking functions; you can make practically anything. This cookbook has many air-frying recipes with step-by-step instructions, easy-to-find ingredients, precise prep/cook time, and serving suggestions.
Air fryers come with practical accessories that enable you to cook any meal you desire. I recommend this appliance because it cooks food in very little time, the cleaning process is straightforward, and the unit is safe to use.
My cookbook has many delicious air-frying recipes, helping you to prepare and cook food for yourself, family and friends. It's so easy to use. Place food in the basket or tray, adjust the temperature and cooking time, and enjoy more time with your loved ones.
I hope you enjoy using this cookbook and that it serves you well for years to come. Thank you for bringing it into your home.

Appendix Air Fryer Cooking Chart

Beef	Temp	Time
Burgers (1/4 Pound)	350°F/175°C	8-12
Filet Mignon (8oz)	400°F/200°C	18-20
Flank Steak (1.5 lbs)	400°F/200°C	10-12
Meatballs (1 inch)	380°F/195°C	7-10
Rib Eye (bone in)	400°F/200°C	10-12
Round Roast (4 lbs)	390°F/200°C	45-55
Sirloin Steak (12oz)	390°F/200°C	9-14

Chicken	Temp	Time
Chicken Whole (3.5 lbs)	350°F/175°C	45-60
Chicken Breast (boneless)	380°F/195°C	12-15
Chicken Breast (bone in)	350°F/175°C	22-25
Chicken Drumsticks	380°F/195°C	23-25
Chicken Thighs (bone in)	380°F/195°C	23-25
Chicken Tenders	350°F/175°C	8-12
Chicken Wings	380°F/195°C	22-25

Fish & Seafood	Temp	Time
Calamari	400°F/200°C	4-5
Fish Fillets	400°F/200°C	10-12
Salmon Fillets	350°F/175°C	8-12
Scallops	400°F/200°C	5-7
Shrimp	370°F/185°C	5-7
Lobster Tails	370°F/185°C	5-7
Tuna Steaks	400°F/200°C	7-10

Pork & Lamb	Temp	Time
Bacon	350°F/175°C	8-12
Lamb Chops	400°F/200°C	8-12
Pork Chops (1" boneless)	400°F/200°C	8-10
Pork Loin (2 lbs)	360°F/180°C	18-21
Rack of Lamb (24-32oz)	375°F/190°C	22-25
Ribs	400°F/200°C	10-15
sausages	380°F/195°C	10-15

Frozen Foods	Temp	Time
Breaded Shrimp	400°F/200°C	8-9
Chicken Burger	360°F/180°C	12-12
Chicken Nuggets	370°F/185°C	10-12
Chicken Strips	380°F/195°C	12-15
Corn Dogs	400°F/200°C	7-9
Fish Fillets	390°F/200°C	10-12
Fish Sticks	390°F/200°C	12-15
French Fries (Thin Cut)	380°F/195°C	12-15
French Fries (Thick Cut)	380°F/195°C	15-17
Hash Brown Patties	380°F/195°C	10-12
Meatballs (1" meatballs)	350°F/175°C	10-12
Meat Pies (1-2 pies)	370°F/185°C	23-25
Mozzarella Sticks	390°F/200°C	7-9
Onion Rings	380°F/195°C	8-10
Pizza	390°F/200°C	5-10
Pizza Rolls	380°F/195°C	7-9
Pot Stickers	390°F/200°C	8-10
Spring Rolls	390°F/200°C	12-15
sweet Potato Fries	380°F/195°C	12-15
Tater Tots	380°F/195°C	15-17

vegetables	Temp	Time
Asparagus	400°F/200°C	5
Beets	400°F/200°C	40
Broccoli Florets	400°F/200°C	6
Brussel Sprouts (halved)	380°F/195°C	12-15
Carrots (1/2" slices)	360°F/180°C	12-15
Cauliflower Florets	400°F/200°C	10-12
Corn on the Cob	390°F/200°C	6-7
Eggplant (1/2" cubes)	400°F/200°C	12-15
Green Beans	500°F/200°C	4-6
Mushrooms	400°F/200°C	4-5
Onions (pearl)	400°F/200°C	8-10
Peppers (whole)	380°F/195°C	8-10
Potatoes (Baby)	390°F/200°C	12-15
Potatoes (wedges)	390°F/200°C	15-18
Potatoes (1" Cubes)	390°F/200°C	12-15
Potatoes (whole)	390°F/200°C	35-45
Squash (1" Cubes)	390°F/200°C	12-15
Sweet Potato (Whole)	380°F/195°C	30-35
Tomatoes (cherry)	400°F/200°C	4-5
zucchini (1/2" sticks)	400°F/200°C	10-12

Printed in Great Britain
by Amazon